Colonel (George Hatton) Colomb

The Prince of Army Chaplains

Colonel (George Hatton) Colomb

The Prince of Army Chaplains

ISBN/EAN: 9783742802309

Manufactured in Europe, USA, Canada, Australia, Japa

Cover: Foto ©Andreas Hilbeck / pixelio.de

Manufactured and distributed by brebook publishing software (www.brebook.com)

Colonel (George Hatton) Colomb

The Prince of Army Chaplains

"THE PRINCE
OF
ARMY CHAPLAINS."

Pseudo St. Peter;
OR,
A REGICIDE'S CAREER.

BY
COLONEL COLOMB,
Author of "For King and Kent, 1648," "Donnington Castle," etc.

"That ignorant stage-player, Hugh Peters."—
WALKER'S *History of Independency.*

LONDON: BURNS & OATES, LIMITED.
NEW YORK, CINCINNATI, CHICAGO: BENZIGER BROTHERS.

PREFACE.

THIS little work on the character and doings[*] of HUGH PETERS (dubbed by the brilliant pen of a living chronicler of "The Great Civil War," THE PRINCE OF ARMY CHAPLAINS) is meant for the edification and entertainment of those persons who are so constituted as to be unable to fall in love with regicides, however saintly they are asserted to have been.

The views of Thomas Carlyle and others are criticised at some length. But the admirers of that writer will be surprised to find in the remarks of the Rev. W. Barry, D.D. (at one of the St. Augustine Memorial meetings), the quotation of a passage of extraordinary beauty, strangely at variance with Thomas Carlyle's usual iconoclastic fervour.

[*] A paper on the same subject was read by the author, some few years ago, at a meeting of the SOCIETY OF ANTIQUARIES, which had a good reception.

CONTENTS.

Chapter I.
Shakespeare's Plays Catholic Literature 1

Chapter II.
An Obscure Member of Shakespeare's Company ... 10

Chapter III.
The Ruin of the Anglican Church 17

Chapter IV.
A Word for James II. 24

Chapter V.
Precursors of Irreconcilables, etc. 29

Chapter VI.
Peters' Early Career 35

Chapter VII.
Peters in New England 46

Chapter VIII.
Peters' Departure from New England 59

Chapter IX.
Godly Reformation begun 67

Chapter X.
Peters and the Great Rebellion ... 77

Chapter XI.
Milton and Peters 91

Chapter XII.
Peters and the First War 105

CONTENTS

Chapter XIII.
Peters and Laud 108

Chapter XIV.
Peters maligns King Charles 112

Chapter XV.
Peters and the King's Murder 117

Chapter XVI.
Rushworth *v.* Allen 126

Chapter XVII.
Peters' Supreme Acts of Treason 134

Chapter XVIII.
"Drogheda Quarter" 147

Chapter XIX.
Peters *in Excelsis* 158

Chapter XX.
Hugh Peters at Dunkirk 164

Chapter XXI.
Peters' Decline and Fall 167

Chapter XXII.
A Record of Salem 175

Chapter XXIII.
Exit Hugh Peters 181

Chapter XXIV.
In Memoriam 186

Appendix A.
Letter of Thomas Peters 195

Appendix B.
Hugh Peters—Extracts and Notes from Mr. Gardiner's "Hist. Gt. Civil War" 196

THE PRINCE OF ARMY CHAPLAINS.

CHAPTER I.

SHAKESPEARE'S PLAYS CATHOLIC LITERATURE.

NEAR the middle of September, 1897, at Hales Place,* near Canterbury, a house once visited by the writer of these pages in search of historical MSS., the Rev. William Barry, D.D., read a remarkable paper, entitled. "Catholic Literature since the Reformation."

"Remarkable" is a word which might be italicised; for the lecturer made more than one striking assertion, and pressed into Catholic service writers one of whom, at least, might very reasonably be thought a mortal enemy.

For, though Edmund Burke and Sir Walter Scott deserve some praise from Catholic critics, few would expect that a "fierce Scotch Puritan" could have been enlisted to fire an opening salvo of honour in behalf of the Holy Catholic Church of pre-Reformation era. Nor

* See "For King and Kent" (1648).

would every one, perhaps, anticipate that the late Mr. Froude, once a kind of patron of extreme Protestant Nonconformity—to judge by certain passages in "Froude's Ireland"—might be found lending energetic assistance to Thomas Carlyle in the matter.

This marvel Dr. Barry revealed; and, lest any might doubt the fact, we append the opening passages of the eloquent divine's address to the audience at Hales Place.

"'Never in all history, in ancient times or modern,' says Mr. Anthony Froude, 'never that we know of, have mankind thrown out of themselves anything so grand, so useful, so beautiful as the Catholic Church once was. . . . Wisdom, justice, self-denial, nobleness, purity, high-mindedness—these are the qualities before which the free-born races of Europe have been content to bow; and in no order of men were such qualities to be found as they were found, six hundred years ago, in the clergy of the Catholic Church. They called themselves the successors of the Apostles. They claimed in their Master's name universal spiritual authority; but they made good their pretensions by the holiness of their lives. They were allowed to rule because they deserved to rule. The Church was essentially democratic, while at the same time it had the monopoly of learning; and all the secular power fell to it which learning, combined with sanctity and assisted by superstition, can bestow' (Froude, 'Short Studies,' I., pp. 51, 53).

"Six hundred years ago all that was visible. Pass another three hundred, and the high mediæval order lay in ruins, or was rapidly falling into the deep. Yet, ere it vanished as a period of the world's history, two men, dwelling far apart—the first Italian, the second English—had given to its outward form and its inward meaning a semblance or embodiment which promises to last until European civilisation is no more. These two were not priests, but laymen, and you have anticipated their names. I cannot but have in my mind's eye Dante and Shakespeare. In them literature attains its sovereign height. 'They dwell apart,' says Carlyle, 'in a kind of royal solitude; none equal, none to succeed them; in the general feeling of the world, a glory as of complete perfection invests these two. They are canonised.' Observe, ladies and gentlemen, that in the judgment of this fierce Scotch Puritan, the 'Divine Comedy' is 'the most remarkable of modern books,' and Dante is acknowledged by him to be the spokesman of the Middle Ages. The thought by which they lived 'stands here,' he tells us, 'in everlasting music'; it is a 'sublime embodiment, or the sublimest, of the soul of Christianity.' But how shall we regard Shakespeare, then? It is Carlyle, again, who joins these two together: 'As in Homer we may still construe old Greece, so in Shakespeare and Dante, after thousands of years, what our modern Europe was in faith and in practice will still be legible. Dante has given us the faith, or soul; Shakespeare, in a not less noble way, has given us the practice, or body.' And still more significant are the words which follow: 'In some sense it may be said that this glorious Elizabethan era, with its Shakespeare as the outcome and flowerage of all that preceded it, is itself attributable to the Catholicism of the Middle Ages. The Christian faith, which was the theme of Dante's song, had produced this practical life which Shakespeare was to sing. For religion then, as it now and always is, was the soul of practice' ('On Heroes,' III., pp. 79, 89, 95)."

Once again Mr. Froude is laid under contribution:

" Let us quote him once more," says Dr. Barry ; "he declares that if Anglican principles are sound, the Reformation was a crime!"

And now as to the heading of this chapter— for we do not pretend to discuss Dante.

From time to time there have been disquisitions on the possible religious opinions of Shakespeare ; and certainly, though by some he has been claimed as an Agnostic, there is nothing in the plays to suggest that he could have had any Puritan sympathies whatever. For, despite the fact that, at rare intervals, certain strong expressions of anti-Papal sentiment appear, there is, upon the whole, little that a staunch Catholic might not have written.

Indeed, it might be supposed that those wonderful masterpieces were composed rather for Catholic than for Protestant audiences ; for, while ardent Reformers had generally little sympathy with the drama, the strong Calvinist was apt to consider the theatre as little better than the ante-chamber of hell.

What are we to think of Fastolfe, Falstaff, or False-staff—actually apologised for on the stage, from being suspected to burlesque the Wickliffite Sir John Oldcastle. Or that the divorced wife of Henry VIII., "the Lily, once the Empress of the field"—not the mother of Elizabeth—is the real heroine of the drama. The ghost of Hamlet's father is a most Catholic ghost. Again, the very name of "Friar" was an offence to Protestant ears. And yet the Friar in *Romeo and Juliet* is a perfect embodiment of all that is amiable, disinterested, virtuous, and pious. Many pages might be filled with reflections of a similar kind.

Although those marvels of wit and wisdom were boasted of as compositions which did not meddle with religious disputations, it is very certain that Protestant rather than Catholic susceptibilities were likely to be roused by much of the language and incidents. Of the individuality of the great dramatist, notwithstanding the recent article in a new encyclopædia, most people must remain in the state of puzzle which Hallam pleaded guilty to, when he practically admits that nothing whatever is known about "the man" Shakespeare.

In vain we seek for light. The five legal signatures, of him who is supposed to have written *currente calamo* (*i.e.*, by inspiration) *and "never blotted a line,"* are all that remain of the assured actual work of that pen. Notwithstanding that since Hallam's day countless

MS. treasures in private houses have been ransacked, not a single letter to or from this almost God-like writer has been discovered. Is it so surprising, then, that some should seek for a new solution of what is certainly a mystery? And that some should even be brought to believe that riddles are hidden under Ben Jonson's prefatory verses, etc., to the folio of 1623; and that traditions, collected many years after Shakespeare's death (by Dryden and those who followed him), although accepted and embodied by Samuel Johnson in the middle of the last century, are, perhaps, not as wholly reliable as Shakespeare's latest biographer imagines? At least a score of curious circumstances seem to some to point to a conclusion that the illiterate atmosphere of Stratford - upon - Avon, where Shakespeare passed his youth,* as well as the obscure position occupied† by him for several years in London, makes it impossible he could have written either the poems and sonnets ascribed to him or those plays which, by the way, came out at first anonymously. Also, that another

* Shakespeare seems to have remained at Stratford-upon-Avon until he was twenty-three.
† Nothing better than looking after gentlemen's horses (outside the theatre) or that of a call-boy.

pen seems more likely to have been more capable of such Olympian flights. It is very true that most people laugh at "The Great Cryptogram," which, as the Rev. Dr. Nicholson, of Leamington, discovered, does not seem to stand the test of serious examination. That, however, does not invalidate many other curious things mentioned by its author, and collected from a variety of reliable sources.

Francis Bacon, when a mere boy, discovered *that too many things were taken for granted;* and, in spite of opposition, laboured until he established his theory, which after ages have fully accepted.

Is it not possible that his master-mind, recoiling from the unreasoning, narrow-minded Geneva doctrine of his day, may have sought in the "despised weed"* of the drama a moral correction of ideas, which could not be openly exposed or contradicted by a man who wished to become a statesman?

Francis Bacon, who was obliged—probably very much against his will—to sit and listen to Travers on Sunday evenings at the Temple, knew very well in what trouble Richard Hooker involved himself in his disputation with the

* "In a despised weed I have sought the good of all mankind."—BACON.

rising sect, and how ready multitudes were to heap abuse upon any who had the least charity for Catholics, respect for Catholicism, or doubts of the infallibility of Calvin.

The plays of Shakespeare are entirely hostile to the petrifying ideas which came from Geneva. They are full of the same wisdom and philosophy which are found in Bacon's acknowledged works—containing actual close paraphrases of Bacon's language; and yet neither Shakespeare's plays nor Shakespeare are in any way alluded to in the known works of Bacon.* Notwithstanding a recent article in the *Quarterly*, we should not be surprised if ere long persons calling themselves "literary" may cease to scorn the "Baconians" and to mock at their theories, although the latest biographer of Shakespeare so valiantly takes up the cudgels against them.

In the meantime, the rather startling appropriation of Shakespeare's plays as "Catholic literature" by the astute lecturer at Hales Place must be accepted as a kind of new discovery.

* The liberality of Bacon in matters of faith may be suspected from many passages in his works. In the essay on "Superstition" we find the following: "It were better to have no opinion of God at all than such an opinion as is unworthy of Him . . . There is a superstition in avoiding superstition when men think to go furthest from the superstition formerly received." (The last paragraph seems to be a direct cut at the Puritans.)

CHAPTER II.

An Obscure Member of Shakespeare's Company.

If the "Shakespeare Plays" are to be claimed as Catholic literature, it must also be recorded that a humble member of the Company of Players who performed therein became a very important agent in the temporary destruction of the new ecclesiastical system first instituted by Henry VIII., which goes under the name of the "Reformed Church." A Life of Hugh Peters, or, as he signed himself, "Peter," mentions the circumstance that he had played the part of "jester, or, rather, fool" in "Shakespeare's Company of Players"; and, though a whole school of modern historians, both American and English, interested in rehabilitating the regicides of 1648, affect to disbelieve it, there surely is nothing improbable in the tradition.

That Peters had performed when William Shakespeare was actually connected with "the Globe," or "Blackfriars," is, however, not asserted; and, indeed, the biographer of Peters places his appointment at a period subsequent to Shakespeare's death.

From most descriptions, until we come to modern apologists, quoting chiefly New England authorities, we must conclude him to have been a buffoon and pulpit jester—a character not altogether unknown amongst better men than "Cromwell's mad chaplain," who, in meeting-houses and even in churches, have treated their congregations to *extempore* Calvinistic discourses,* as Peters did.

Some of Peters' pious orations will be briefly alluded to in their proper place later on. From his effrontery and garrulity, it is very probable that during his theatrical career he would have come under the censure of Hamlet, in his advice to players, for an unseemly employment of "gag."

The whole story of Hugh Peters, as told by Yonge, severe, sarcastic, and contemptuous though it be, notwithstanding exaggeration, has an air of truth and probability in it. Of perjury,

* And not confined to that school, *teste* Dean Swift.

treason, and regicide* Peters was clearly guilty. Other "indiscretions" (which "the Saints" would try to conceal) seem not improbable accompaniments. Yonge had a powerful pen, and a considerable share of wit; and we are bound to believe, as his evidence was accepted at the trial—and, like other evidence at the trial, imperfectly rebutted by Peters—that he had a fair knowledge of what he was talking about (though not always perfectly well informed). At all events, we may suppose he had as much knowledge of his subject as writers like Mr. Felt, with an opposite bias, who lived two centuries later. Mr. S. R. Gardiner, the painstaking and voluminous chronicler of the "Great Civil War," having so exalted an opinion of Cromwell, is naturally, on the *noscitur ex sociis* principle, obliged to be a justifier of Peters. Peters' biographer, in a recent monumental work not yet completed, also gives a very glowing account of his character and actions which sympathisers with King and Cavalier can by no means endorse.

It is summed up in the following passage: "An examination of the career and writings

* *Vide* Mr. Gardiner's remarks on Peters' active assistance in persuading hesitating regicides to sign the warrant for the execution of Charles I.

of Peters shows him to have been an honest, upright, and genial man, whose defects of taste and judgment explain much of the odium which he incurred, but do not justify it."

After such an expression of opinion, it is not wonderful that Dr. W. Yonge is anathematised by the same distinguished writer, although much of what Yonge says is substantiated by him. The accusations of Yonge, supported as they are by a variety of evidence, are, however, not so easily demolished. Peters was deeply concerned in the murder of his King—surely not a very creditable circumstance in the career of an Anglican divine (!) Yonge bore witness at the trial of Peters, and his evidence was corroborated by others.

We may be very certain that the man who received at the hands of the supreme regicide the highest appointment in the "Cromwellian Church," and who was always favoured by him, must have been, as was universally believed, deep in those counsels of blood which enabled the ex-tithe farmer to seize supreme power and sit, like Macbeth, in high place with assassins * to serve him at his need. It is not difficult to believe that the restless, meddling Peters, may

* The High Court of "Injustice" (!)

have been the important factor that Yonge describes—and that others described—in the desperate plots of the hour, forming nothing less than a member of the triumvirate of which the two leaders were Cromwell and Ireton—Fairfax, the perplexed tool of the plotters, of course, scarcely counts as a factor, though he was the nominal head of the Rebel army. (There were, of course, scores of mad Saints assisting.) Any desperate intrigue at such a crisis as that which led up to " Pride's Purge " was possible. Therefore, we maintain that in the account of what went on at Windsor, and in Coleman Street, and elsewhere, the story of Peters airing his opinions about what ought to be done to " Charles Stuart " must be accepted, not only as possible, but as probable in the extreme.

If the remains of Parliamentarian government had not been destroyed by " Pride's Purge," and if the establishment of the " High Court of Justice " by the Rump (or forty tyrants as they were called) had not presently succeeded—the lives of Cromwell and Ireton, and many other leading Roundheads, would have certainly been in deadly peril. The bold Judge Jenkins—whom they put in the Tower, and kept in confinement till the Restoration for saying so—plainly told them that the law would hang them all.

Had a restoration followed the Isle of Wight Treaty, it seems likely that neither the King nor his ministers, whoever they might have been, would have been able to save them from the penalties of high treason. For King and Cavalier had now become popular with the vast majority of the nation, groaning under the tyrannies of soldiers and committee men.

The situation was desperate; and it seems rather doubtful if Macaulay was altogether right in saying that the judicial murder of Charles was "an error," though it was certainly "a crime," and a monstrous one—even in self-defence—on the part of men who pretended to be the salt of the earth, and to be guided by the precepts of the Gospel.

The sad spectre of PETER(s), ex-clown or fool of "Shakespeare's Company of Players" — forsworn Anglican priest and regicide preacher—rises strangely above the ruins of Throne and Church! It will be noted by-

and-bye that this pseudo-St. Peter, besides being the spiritual head of what we may call Cromwell's Church,* was found at the Restoration to be in charge of "The King's Library," as well as of that of the decapitated Archbishop.

An Obscure Member of Shakespeare's Company.—In repeating at the end of this chapter the words which are placed at the beginning, how incredibly strange it appears that we know infinitely† more of him than we do of the man who was "not for an Age, but for all Time"!

* No wonder that William Coddington, from New England, seeing Peters established at Whitehall and in possession of Laud's Library, as well as being head of the "Tryers," should be "merry with Peters, and call him *the Archbishop of Canterbury*, in regard of his attendance of ministers and gentlemen" (see "National Biography").

† See the voluminous references in the "National Biography," quoted by Mr. C. H. Firth.

CHAPTER III.

THE RUIN OF THE ANGLICAN CHURCH.

WAS the Anglican Church really, for the time, destroyed by the Rebellion which commenced with the murder of Strafford and of Laud, and culminated with that of the King "under the forms of law"?

It is not inexpedient to ask and to answer that question, in consequence of the almost absolute oblivion of the sufferings of King Charles and his supporters, resulting from the persistent attempts, for the last seventy years or so, to glorify the "party of movement," as by some the "root and branch" reform party is called.

There is also another reason why the persecution, or rather the complete abolition of the Anglican Church for about fifteen years at least, should no longer be mentioned—which is, that the tactics of Church defence are wholly changed since old Toryism disappeared.

Nothing could be more singular at the great Church meeting, some few years ago, which was attended by so many eminent politicians and divines, than the unanimity which precluded the smallest allusion on the part of any speaker to that army of martyrs, with King Charles and Archbishop Laud at its head, which had faced and suffered misfortune and ruin in various forms—doleful imprisonment; long years of exile; slavery in tropical climes; death in appalling shapes—rather than violate their oaths, or be false to their creed.

Strange, that while our ecclesiastical system seemed to Churchmen to be menaced with the fate of two hundred and forty years previously —*i.e.*, of being destroyed by a Parliamentary decree—no mention of heroic predecessors should have been made!

Altered circumstances, however, it is easy to see, rendered it impossible. And Church defence was based then, as it is now, and will be in the future, upon the grounds that neither Parliament nor individual has any right to touch ecclesiastical property.

However just and reasonable that argument may be, it is very certain that if a serious assault should ever be made upon the Church

THE RUIN OF THE ANGLICAN CHURCH 19

of England, its revenues will be the one thing which the enemy will determine to seize ; and, as in the time of the Great Rebellion, the seizure will be made, or at all events attempted, without the shadow of a scruple.

When the clergy by common consent—or rather, from never thinking at all about the matter, which is of no practical concern—seem to ignore the history of the past, it is not surprising that a vast number of laymen—unless they are convinced Republicans or political dissenters—who are, indeed, well versed in the particulars—will find much novelty, or perhaps will receive with absolute incredulity, accounts of what happened in King Charles's time to "the Establishment."

That story is not to be found in such works as "Green's History of the English People,"* or in the eulogies of the heroic men who went forth to fight, "with the Bible in one hand, and the sword in the other "(!)

And, indeed, though the matter is of immense importance, most modern histories say little about those antetypes of the Jacobin clubs,

---

* That very erudite and distinguished light of literature, the late Dr. Brewer, in the *Quarterly Review*, many years ago, lamented the immense sale which this work had, considering its tendencies are mischievous.

called County Committees. These, with the Grand Metropolitan Committees, made their appearance early in the Great Rebellion with respectable, or rather, eminent names on the lists—to be changed eventually into conclaves of obscure personages, who did not hesitate to do sad and dirty work, which they found very profitable.

These tribunals got power from the Long Parliament to divide the sheep from the goats, separating the community into two classes, the " well - affected " and the " malignants " or " delinquents." The loyal clergy were by these soon subjected to increased persecution ; and when the Directory was established in 1644-5, after the murder of Laud, were given the option of breaking their oaths of allegiance, supremacy, and conformity, or of being deprived of their preferments.

To their everlasting honour, the vast majority refused to abandon their King and their Church, and either went into holes and corners for safety, or became chaplains in the Royal army, or in some cases, such as that of Hudson, actual soldiers.

The cathedrals were gutted, plundered, and more or less desecrated. The parish churches generally shared a like fate—though the poor loyal people sometimes managed to protect them against the decrees of Committees and Parliament. The simple possession of a prayer-book rendered a subject liable to the charge of delinquency, and to two years' imprisonment.

The "Bishop's lands" (as well as all other ecclesiastical property) were confiscated; and, at length, even the tithes were appropriated by Cromwell during his Protectorate—who, while affecting to create a "godly" ministry, took good care that they should be supporters of his Government. Among other changes, the church organs were generally either destroyed or taken down to be set up—as a foreigner records in 1659—in taverns, where jigs and secular tunes were played on them. In the churches where "superstitious" monuments, and also baptismal fonts, altars, and altar-rails (the hated invention of Archbishop Laud) had been demolished, and much window-glass smashed, a self-elected Independent would occasionally officiate (after, the fashion of the incident described in "Woodstock"), and preach an ignorant, fanatical, or blood-thirsty discourse.

A striking picture of Church government

by "the Saints," during the Interregnum, is given by Mr. Freshfield, in his remarkable illustrations of some City churches (published some few years ago), where the "godly" had it all their own way.*

The book called "Walker's Sufferings of the Clergy" probably gives a very incomplete account of the afflictions suffered by the loyal Anglican divines.

As we said before, the present Anglican clergy are generally somewhat ignorant of what happened to their predecessors in that sad time of trial, and are often found quite ready to quote the popular view of the chief Anglican martyr, learnt from popular histories, which is embodied in the oft-repeated remark: "But then, you know Charles I. was such a liar."†

The Nonconformists, however, are much better instructed in *their* Church history, and are sufficiently proud of the glorious (though wickedly forced) exodus of the two thousand (?) ministers who refused, after the Restoration, to

* See his discourse on St. Stephen's, Coleman Street.

† "Some historians," says the philosophical Hume, who was not a party man, "have rashly questioned the good faith of this Prince. But for this reproach, the most malignant scrutiny of his conduct, which in every circumstance is now thoroughly known, affords not any reasonable foundation," etc. (see any *old* edition of "Hume's History").

accept Royal supremacy, Episcopacy, Common Prayer, surplice, etc., etc.

Our conclusion must, we think, be agreed to by all who really know historical facts, that *the Anglican Church was temporarily effaced by the Great Rebellion.*

The Rev. Dr. Barry quotes, as we have seen, Mr. Froude's apothegm, "*That if Anglican principles are sound the Reformation was a crime.*"

If it was indeed a crime, it met with a signal punishment in the years between 1640 and 1660. Anglicanism was, and is by far, the most important outcome and offspring of the Reformation.

If the revival of Anglicanism at the almost miraculous Restoration in 1660—bought by the sufferings and blood of its martyrs—had not taken place, undoubtedly the REFORMATION would have been (once more to apply Macaulay's phrase in altered fashion), "not only a crime, but an error." It is quite fair, we think, to make this assertion. Protestant sects, numerous enough, as every one knows, at present, would long ere this have reached a fabulous figure.*

* Bacon believed that the multiplication of sects led to Atheism.

CHAPTER IV.

A Word for James II.

MANY and heavy are the censures which have been passed upon the ex-Monarch of England, who left the throne vacant, and made way for the Dutch grandson of Charles I., whom Jacobites called "the Usurper."

Not only the historians who have written his memoirs, but also the courtiers of the great King,* who so magnanimously received and entertained his brother in distress, sneered at the man who sacrificed his Royal inheritance for a Mass.

Obloquy, we say, has been sufficiently heaped upon James II.; and yet, was not his blamable conduct, under the circumstances, to a man with strong religious convictions, natural enough? Like his father, Charles I., and his grandfather, James, he,

* As Voltaire remarked, most histories of this King were composed by his personal enemies ("Siècle de Louis XIV.")

no doubt, fully accepted the idea imbibed from Scripture, that Kings were under the special protection of God Almighty—a doctrine which the rebellious Puritans, though believing in the verbal inspiration of a Holy Book, chose to ignore in a simple and practical manner.

It is possible that even Charles II., notwithstanding his careless life and apparently thoughtless conduct, had something of the same strong belief. Both of them, however, had peculiar experiences.

They had learnt the fact that, notwithstanding the Divine protection promised in Holy Writ, their sincerely pious and virtuous parent, the native and hereditary King of England, and acknowledged head of the Anglican Church, was put to death like a criminal by barbarous and vindictive enemies.

If Charles II. appeared to have no particular religion, when his end came it was proved by his sending for Huddleston that he *had* decided views; but not those of the Church of which he was the hereditary head.

Is it not likely that the blamable conduct of James II. might be explained somewhat in the following manner: He saw his relative, Louis

XIV., the so-called *Dieu-donné*, ruling in France with power and glory, something after the model of kings in Scripture history, a Darius or Ahasuerus, who could do what he liked, whose splendour eclipsed that of Solomon; and who, for a long period at least, had been idolised by the majority of his subjects.

Everything was flourishing — arms, arts, literature, the drama, trade, commerce; and, besides great generals, statesmen, and poets—pious, learned, and eloquent divines.

Did not James then contrast his poor father's troubled reign, sad trials, and tragic end with the apparently fixed and almost miraculous greatness and prosperity of his cousin?*

If both Charles and James rested more or less on that powerful relative's support (a thing for which they have been severely censured), was it not partly because he *was* their relative—but chiefly because Louis appeared to be under actual visible protection from on high.

It was very likely to appear to James and to Charles both—without the persuasive hints of "Jesuits" or interested devotees—that the Reformation was, in modern *parlance*, all a

---

* Also connected by the marriage of his sister Henrietta to the brother of Louis XIV.

mistake. Henry VIII., under these circumstances, they might consider an ecclesiastical usurper, and their poor father a deluded, though pious and virtuous Prince, suffering for the sins of his predecessors.

Charles II., an easy-going, good-natured man of the world, accepted things as they were; and, finding that he could not govern, contented himself with the pursuit of pleasure.

But was not James probably convinced in his own mind that the only way to make England great, and himself powerful, was to undo as far as possible the error or crime of the Reformation and bring back the Old Faith?

He, as we said before, like his Protestant father, Charles I., no doubt believed that the Ruler of the Universe *was on his side;* and, when all his designs and labours failed, was probably vastly surprised—more surprised than his father was when he found himself on the scaffold in front of his own house (!)

For Charles had the consolation that he was a martyr to the liberties of his subjects—an idea not so much without foundation as his hostile critics and enemies suppose. His refusal to recognise the military despotism consequent upon the destruction of Parliament, and to condone the plunder of the Church by accepting the position of a puppet-King, will one day be remembered to his lasting honour.

That James II. was surprised as well as disappointed with the turn events took in 1689 will account for his vacillating conduct, not only in his military operations in Ireland, but also in the manner in which he left "the throne vacant." We miss the gallant spirit he had formerly shown, both as a sailor and as a soldier.*

---

* To throw the great seal into the Thames was probably not an act of malice, but of confusion and fear. He probably remembered at that time the way in which the King's name and authority had been used against the King's person and interests in his father's case.

CHAPTER V.

Precursors of Irreconcilables, etc.

Sir Henry Maine, in his eminently curious and pregnant remarks upon " Popular Government," proclaims certain *obiter dicta* which may well startle the complacency of some modern historians, as well as those who commend their exhaustive literary labours, or are led captive by their plausible arguments.

Alluding to Cromwell and the Independents, he describes them as "the true precursors of the modern irreconcilables" (!) ("Age of Progress," p. 135).

That Hugh Peters was one of those "precursors" must be admitted by those who read either Yonge's or Felt's account of him.

Indeed, Peters (or Peter) left behind him an unction which is vaguely present, not only throughout the whole history of the Northern States of America, but also in the course of the Great French Revolution and Reign of Terror.

Both the Great American Revolt in the last

century, and the consequent destruction of the Monarchy of France, were to a large extent copies of the Great Civil War in our own country.

Without going into particulars, it ought to be sufficient for the moment to remember that the leaders of the American Revolt *searched the folios of Rushworth for precedents.*

It is very true that the Revolt ended (chiefly through the labours of the wise Hamilton) in an attempt to copy, not the British Constitution, but the actual Government which they were revolting from, namely (as far as practicable), that of the detested George III.!* As for the Great French Revolution, it was a more complete copy of the Great Rebellion of 1640 *et seq.* The revolting Americans could not capture "obstinate George III.," try him by a High Court of Justice, and cut off his head (a thing which they would at the time have had the greatest pleasure in doing). But the French Jacobins were able not only to "execute the villainy" they had been taught by the English regicides, but also "to better the instruction." They cut off the head of the

---

* Sir Henry Maine seems to have been the first to notice this fact. Probably, even now, few Americans have grasped it.

Queen as well as the head of the King, and, in addition to various other much to be lamented acts, so arranged matters as to inflict lasting injuries on their country. We have already alluded to the fact that the Jacobin clubs were evidently copies of our Great Rebellion confiscating committees. And was not NAPOLEON, when he made his grand *coup* of the 18th Brumaire, a copy of CROMWELL, though at the moment he was copying, he expressly said he *was not (!)* Of course, NAPOLEON was not a Jacobin, and the 18th Brumaire was far more justifiable than "Pride's Purge." There was no pretext of protecting "the poor people of God" (who, indeed, in our rebellion and civil war, had shown they were pretty well able to protect as well as to enrich themselves), by suppressing a Parliament and murdering a King. NAPOLEON was accepted as—and, no doubt, honestly believed himself to be—the restorer of order to a distracted and disintegrated nation. *Passim* we may remark that Bonaparte's military victories were far more excusable and much more extraordinary than Oliver's, as his talent as a statesman and a ruler were beyond all comparison greater.

Cromwell may also be said to be not only

the precursor also of Napoleon III., as regards his assault upon the French Chambers in 1851, but of scores or perhaps hundreds of " Saviours of the People" in the South American continent.

Perhaps in those politically volcanic regions the *Agreement of the People*, or other crude inventions of the Independents in 1647, may have been tried and possibly found wanting.

Strange, weird jokes sometimes seem to be naturally evolved from portentous events. That 3rd of September, for instance. How singular it was that the illustrious rebel should die on the anniversary of that day that he conquered: Ireland (Siege of Drogheda, 1649), Scotland (Battle of Dunbar, 1650), England (Battle of Worcester, 1651)! Odd, too, the recorded prediction of his high priest and "mad chaplain"!

Peters, before the King was beheaded, preached before Cromwell and the military and other Saints a (three hours'?) sermon in St. Margaret's Church. His text was, "Bind your kings with chains, and your nobles with fetters of iron."

"Moses," said he (meaning Cromwell*),

---

* Peters again alluded to Cromwell as Moses in his funeral sermon in 1658. The text was "My servant Moses is dead."

"shall lead the people out of Egyptian bondage. But how is this to be done? That," said he, "has not yet been revealed to me." He now covered his eyes with his hands, and bending down buried his head in the pulpit cushion. After a little while he started up, and cried out: "Now I have it by revelation! This army must root up monarchy, NOT ONLY IN ENGLAND, BUT IN FRANCE —and other kingdoms round about. But," added he, "there are foolish citizens in our Jerusalem" (meaning, no doubt, the Presbyterian clergy; who, being satisfied with the King's Newport concessions, petitioned against his trial and execution) "who for a little trading and profit would have Christ crucified" (pointing to the soldiers) "and that Great Barabbas of Windsor released!"

"Not only in England, but in France!!" In a more superstitious age than ours, this revelation of the "mad" army chaplain would have been set down as communicated by the powers below! "*Not only in England, but in France!*" For does not this seem a forecast of the important copy of the crime of 1648 [*]

[*] O. S.

—seeing that it applies pretty exactly to the murder of Louis XIII. and Marie Antoinette —one hundred and forty-four years later!

And, moreover, once again we see another phantom, PETER—corner-stone of mischief! There is at least a kind of shadow of his name in that of the High Priest of Revolution and Manager of THE TERROR—need we name "the incorruptible" Maximilian ROBESPIERRE!!

CHAPTER VI.

Peters' Early Career.

Hugh Peters, or Peter, was born at Fowey, then called Foy, in Cornwall, in 1599. His mother was a Treffry, a family still represented in that county. It is said that Peters' father was a merchant, though some say a dyer, and that he was driven from Antwerp on account of his religion. His original name was not Peters, but Dyckwood according to some accounts. Hugh Peters went to Cambridge at the age of fourteen; and is said to have obtained the degree of B.A. in 1617, and that of M.A. in 1622. As Cromwell entered Cambridge on the day that Shakespeare died, April 23rd, 1616, Peters may have been known to Cromwell there. It is said that Peters was dismissed from Cambridge for misconduct.* This accu-

---

* One account says that among his delinquencies he was charged with poisoning deer. This looks like an improvement on a Shakespearian legend. (But if Milton is supposed to have got into trouble with his superiors, why not Peters also?)

sation, as well as many others, is set down as slander by New England writers: it at least wants confirmation.

Peters had a brother called Thomas, who was a Calvinistic preacher, and was driven from Cornwall by the Royalists. He was a sincere Roundhead, as may be seen by a letter (*vide* Appendix A.), which also reveals that, like his brother, he had an eye to business. While talking religion and treason he refers to mining interests. " Hugh Peters, coming to London," says Dr. William Yonge, who professed to know him *intus et cute* (having entertained Peters in his house for many weeks), "joined a common society of players: when, after venting his frothy inventions, he had a greater call to a higher promotion, namely to be a jester, or rather a fool, in Shakespeare's Company of Players." But having heard a sermon at St. Faith's, where he had apparently "gone to scoff," he "remained to pray"; and, to use the words of Yonge, "he deserted his companions and employments, and returning to his chamber near Fleet Conduit, continued between hope and despair a year or more." It was at this period, no doubt, if not before, that Hugh Peters adopted Calvinistic views.

A gentleman (most likely Winthrop, or one of Winthrop's friends) got him "settled in a free school in Essex." "He pays court to one Mistress Read, a widow with two or three hundred pounds a year. Dr. Yonge describes how he won the widow's fancy, by the help of humorous grimaces learnt upon the stage; and obtained possession of the prize by a more than smart trick.* The lady was the widow of Edmund Read, of Wickford, Essex, and mother of Colonel Thomas Read, afterwards Governor of Stirling, and a partisan of Monk at the Restoration. Mrs. Edmund Read also had a daughter, Elizabeth, who, about the year 1635, married the younger Winthrop, Governor of Connecticut. This Elizabeth was therefore a step-daughter of Peters.

Peters seems to have returned to London and set up as a preacher. His account of himself at this time (see "Peters' Legacy," said to be written just before his execution) is as follows:

"To Sepulchre's (church) I was brought by a very strange Providence; for, preaching be-

---

* Mr. Gardiner, in Vol. II. of his "History of the Great Civil War," takes great pains in a footnote to disprove Yonge's story by calling in question other statements of Dr. Yonge (see Appendix B.)

fore at another place, and a young man receiving some good, would not be satisfied but I must preach at Sepulchre's, once monthly for the good of his friends; in which he got his end (if I might not show vanity), and he allowed thirty pounds per annum to that lecture, but his person was unknown to me. He was a chandler, and died a good man and member of Parliament.* At this lecture the resort grew so great that it contracted envy and anger; though I believe above a hundred every week were persuaded from sin to Christ. There were six or seven thousand† hearers, and the circumstance fit for such good work."

Peters does not mention here whether he preached against the bishops, as other lecturers did.‡ Yonge, however, settles that question by a positive assertion, and it is, of course, corroborated by Peters' subsequent headstrong career. He had been ordained by Bishop Mountain; and took the oaths of allegiance, supremacy, and canonical obedience. Of this last fact there is not the least doubt; for it was

* One of the "Rump," no doubt.

† This seems to be one of Peters' "spread-eagle" assertions; for the church could not possibly hold such a multitude.

‡ At an early period, according to papers in the Record Office, he distinguished himself by keeping a fast on St. Andrew's Day, and praying for the conversion of Henrietta Maria.

proved by papers found amongst Laud's after the Restoration. Similar evidence appeared as to the oaths taken by Marshal, Nye and Goodwin, also other renegade Churchmen.

Peters, according to Yonge, about this time got a great reputation amongst the women as a preacher. This is very likely; for some years later he was known to be one of the most successful "thimble-and-bodkin" orators.*

Mr. Freshfield draws a profound conclusion in his incisive commentaries on those London Parish Records—which he so strangely and happily rescued, when they were on the point of being destroyed as worthless rubbish—namely, that when in Elizabeth's reign "the lecturer" was admitted into the Church, the authority of the Bishop was undermined.

Dr. Yonge accounts for the sudden departure of Peters from the surroundings where he was so popular, to Holland, by chronicling one of the stories set down by Winthrop and other New England Fathers as scandalous—though very constantly asserted to be true—viz., that he had some intrigue with a citizen's wife. He became a preacher

* From what we read of him in his New England career he was a diligent "house-to-house" visitor.

at Rotterdam,* supplanting a certain Dr. Bartlett by unfair means (according to Yonge), where he remained several years. Here again the sarcastic pen of Yonge attacks the reputation of the priest of revolution, and sets down a tale which reminds us of an incident in Molière's comedy of *Tartuffe*. A lady, called Franklyn, with whom Peters had been too intimate, at length complains of him to her husband; whereupon Mr. Franklyn "entertains Peters with crab-tree sauce."

Is it not possible that Peters may be the original of Tartuffe? It is certain that Peters was at Dunkirk in 1658, and that he was there well known to Cardinal Mazarin (query, if not to Louis XIV.) and other eminent personages. Even Molière himself may have seen and studied him. Peters had several interviews with Mazarin, meddling in State business —which was a common practice of his, or rather, constant employment. Lockhart complains to Thurloe of this; but at the same time sends Peters back to England with communications of importance for the private

---

* Whether Peters' wife accompanied him to Rotterdam, or what became of her, seems difficult to discover. Mr. Felt, his vindicator, does not clear up the mystery. She seems, at all events, not to have gone with him to New England.

ear of Thurloe or of the Protector. The character of Tartuffe is known to be the creation of Molière, and not a copy of any other dramatist's work.

A few years later (1663) Yonge dedicates his memoirs of Hugh Peters to Henrietta Maria, ex-Queen of England; and on the title-page of the work Hugh Peters is called "that grand Impostor." It is plain, therefore, that this volume would be known at the Court of Louis XIV.; and it is suggestive that the hero of Molière's comedy is also called "The Impostor" (*Tartuffe, l'Imposteur*).

It is beyond dispute that Peters was a born comedian, or naturally "funny man."

The following criticism from a French pen, being somewhat *à propos*, is here inserted:

"Le Tartuffe," says *La Harpe*, "est ingrat et l'est d'une manière horrible; mais les grimaces de son hypocrisie, et ses expressions dévotes melées, à ses entreprises, amoureuses donnent à son rôle une tournure comique."

We may remark that the regicide origin of the *rôle* of Tartuffe (if it was inspired by a study of Peters) would naturally not be much mentioned in the Court of the Grand Monarque, however well it might be known. There had been the rebellion of the Fronde as well as the English " troubles."

If Yonge's tales of Peters were "scandalous," as Winthrop says, they may at least have been believed by Henrietta Maria, who had little reason to think well of the Cromwellian high priest.

The ex-Queen's daughter, the charming Henriette d'Orléans—ancestress of so many kings and princes—was, no doubt, the original of the interesting *Henriette* in Molière's *Femmes Savantes*.

The army of modern historians, of course, agree with Winthrop; but we should like it to be explained why it is unlikely that this perjured turn-coat Anglican clergyman, who was found guilty of conspiracy to murder his unfortunate Sovereign, and had apparently worked hard to destroy both the Church and the State for many years, should be quite immaculate in other respects.*

It is, of course, on the principle of *noscitur a sociis*, necessary to whitewash the man who

---

* Peters would never reply to the frequent public accusations brought against him until near his death, when he professed to his daughter that he was immaculate. The modern historians think nothing of the condemnation pronounced by a mass of Restoration writers, such as Dr. Barwick, nor of Burnett, who echoed them.

was a familiar friend of "the Great Protector." But the Great Protector, who had no scruple in murdering, by a method not too brave, the "native hereditary" King of England—*whom he had at least three times solemnly vowed to protect*—had other intimate friends who by no means possessed the virtues of Scipio or Joseph. Harry Marten, long an associate—reproached by Cromwell with opprobrious words on April 20th, 1653—was for many years mocked at, in hundreds of diurnals and pamphlets, for the grossest misconduct. Nor does Pym appear to have been thought a very rigid saint, except in opposing the "Book of Sports," and in his great zeal for reformation of Church and State, though he was the bosom friend of the irreproachable John Hampden.

Was even Cromwell himself quite above suspicion?

The censorious were scandalised at his intimacy with a certain Lady D——, a lady of some attractions; and when this intimacy had to be dropped, in consequence of hostile criticisms, he is reported to have consoled himself by paying court to the wife of an officer of the name of Lambert: not, perhaps, the general and fictitious Lord, but possibly some connection.* The fact

* See that extremely well-written and interesting modern work called "Royalty Restored."

is that "the Saints" during that period, so long as offenders were earnest for what they termed "the faith," and devotedly hostile to the Royalist cause, thought somewhat lightly of even serious misconduct, or at least assisted in concealing the offence. " Tell it not in Gath, lest the ungodly triumph," was a sentiment in vogue.

A time may possibly arrive—for fashions in literature, like other fashions, are subject to change—when the English regicides shall take their proper place. Though they have been much written up, as we have already remarked, for about seventy years or so, the glamour of the Royalist cause has not yet been quite destroyed : and it is probable that people with a strong sense of humour—which biographers of regicides do not always seem to possess—are not invariably quite ready to fall down and worship the gilded images which have been set up.

CHAPTER VII.

PETERS IN NEW ENGLAND.

PETERS, after the escapade mentioned—whether slanderous or otherwise—is described by Yonge as "falling distracted," and continuing so for three years, after which his friends provided him with five hundred pounds, and he went to New England. It is to be observed that the New Englanders admit that the climate of Holland did not agree with him.

"Mr. Peters, pastor of the English Church at Rotterdam," says Winthrop ("Life and Letters of J. Winthrop"), "being persecuted by the English Ambassador, . . . and *not having had his health there many years*, consulted with the ministers about his removal."

While in Holland Peters seems to have been in communication with some great Puritan leaders, Warwick, the Lords Say and Brooke, and Sir Arthur Hazelrigg, etc., also with the

Winthrops; and he was, in point of fact, one of the founders of the Massachusetts Bay Company. He was, says one account, one of the signers of the instructions to Endicott, the first governor, in 1628.

It is noteworthy—as being in harmony with Peters' later career as a combatant military chaplain—that while in Holland he hired Lyon Gardiner, a soldier engineer under the Prince of Orange, at one hundred pounds per annum, as Professor of Fortification for the New England settlement in behalf of the Company. This fact also shows the influence he had already acquired.

Peters' arrival in New England, and who some of his companions were, is noted in the early records of the Colony.

His advent is, indeed, recorded with a flourish of trumpets. His reforming zeal and pulpit success no doubt commended him to the heads of the reforming party in England. No doubt, then, that he was well introduced to "the Fathers," and at once took up a leading position in Massachusetts.

"This year (1635)," says one account, "came over that famous servant of Christ, Mr. Hugh Peters. He was called to office by the Church of Christ at Salem, their former pastor, the Rev. Mr. Higginson* having ended his labours resting in the Lord."

In a "Journal of the Colony" we note: "1635.—Sir Henry Vane, Junr., arrived in New England . . . and Hugh Peters chosen pastor of Salem."

In the book called "The Life and Letters of J. Winthrop," by a descendant, the author says Peters "arrived in the *Abigail* with young J. Winthrop" (afterwards Governor of Connecticut) "and Thomas Shepard — soon to be known and ever afterwards remembered as the eminent minister of Cambridge."

"The other new-comer in the *Abigail*," says the same Winthrop, quoting early accounts, "was one Mr. Harry Vane, son to the Comptroller of the Household" (to Charles I.) "Being called to the obedience of the Gospel, he forsook the honours and preferments of the Court to enjoy the ordinances of Christ in their purity here."

It is curious to remember that "the younger Vane," while in England, was troubled in his

---

* It should have been mentioned, however, that the heretic, Roger Williams, had filled the place for a short time.

mind because he could not persuade any clergyman to administer the sacrament *standing**
instead of sitting : *kneeling*, for a good Puritan, was, of course, out of the question.

The Colonial accounts assert that Sir Harry Vane, Senr., disapproved of his son's proceedings. He appears to have referred the matter for the King's decision ; and Charles I., upon consideration of all "circumstances, commanded him to send him hither, and gave him leave for three years to stay."

Winthrop takes pains to specify that Sir Harry Vane, Senr., was far from being " godly."

Apparently, Thomas Shepard, an intimate friend of Peters, either then or afterwards came over, not in the *Abigail*, but in the *Defence*.†
He succeeded Thomas Hooke as minister of Cambridge, New England.

Shepard, like Peters, though to a lesser extent, became an important figure in the new colony. He was born at Towcester, in England, on the day of "the Gunpowder Plot," and was educated at Cambridge University. He had been ordained priest and deacon in England. He himself describes at some length

* Mentioned in " The Strafford Papers."
† Perhaps the two ships arrived about the same time.

his inhibition by Laud, then Bishop of London, and the manifest anger of that prelate, who had conceived a prejudice against him. The inhibition took place on the 16th December, 1630.

"You prating coxcomb," said Laud to Shepard; "do you think all the learning is in your brain? . . . I charge you that you neither preach, read, marry, bury, nor exercise any ministration or function in any part of my diocese."*

This may by some be thought a tyrannical proceeding, but possibly Bishop Laud had good reasons for his conduct. A remarkable letter from Shepard to his "dear Brother Peters, minister of Christ everywhere," will be found in the "Proceedings of the Soc. Antiq^s.," March 17th, 1887, in which Shepard gives the following definition of his principles: "Toleration of all *upon pretence of conscience; I thank my God, my soul abhors it.*"

In the same letter to Peters, which is dated December 27th, 1645—Shepard's enemy, Laud, having been executed a year or so previously —he says: "We were thinking to desire the A. Bishop's library" (this had been presented

* "Mass. Hist. Coll.," Second Series, Vol. VIII., p. 46.

to Peters),* "and that the Parliament would recompense your labours for public good with something more useful to yourself."

In "Mass. Hist. Coll." we find a list of ministers in New England: "At Cambridge, Master Shepard, pastor; Master Dunster, schoolmaster, with about twenty scholars under him." This was the nucleus of the now well-known Harvard University. Dunster, in 1650, became the first President of it. Probably the office might have been filled by Shepard had he not died the year previously.

"On the 25th May, 1636," the following important circumstance is recorded: "The Governor Vane, Deputy-Governor J. Winthrop, Thomas Dudley, John Haynes . . . Mr. PETERS, and Mr. Shepard are instructed to make a draft of laws agreeable to the Word of God, which may be the fundamentals of the Commonwealth."†

The various records of the North American Colonies of that day contain a mass of notes chronicling isolated facts which are difficult to

---

* Mr. Felt (H. P. 26) quotes an assertion of Archbishop Laud: "All my books at Lambeth were, by order of the House of Commons, taken away and carried I know not whither; but are, it is commonly said, for the use of Peters.

† "Mass. Hist. Coll.," Third Series, Vol. VIII., p. 204.

harmonise. No doubt, future American historians will find in them a mine almost inexhaustible, and "Bancroft's History" may one day be increased to the dimensions of an encyclopædia (!)

It is not easy to discover what became of Peters' (first) wife: she did not go with him to New England. It is instead recorded that Mary Morell accompanied him in the capacity of waiting-maid. The "maid" afterwards seems to have married one Peter Folger. In modern times, to travel with such an attendant would be thought, to say the least, eccentric. We remember hearing a tale of a country curate, who, being invited to stay with the Lord Lieutenant of an English county, was so overcome with the honour conferred upon him that he called upon his Bishop to know "what dress he ought to go in?" "Dress?" replied the Bishop, "why, that you are in now, of course; a clergyman's dress. But," added the Bishop, "I should advise you—for you will find it a great comfort—to take a servant with you."

The curate thanked his Lordship and departed. Next day he arrived at the Lord Lieutenant's mansion in a four-wheeler. It happened that most of the guests, including a number of sporting gentlemen, were near the hall door. They were considerably amused on beholding that the poor curate had brought his parlour-maid with him (!).

A charitable pamphlet says that Peters sold his wife as a slave to the West Indies (Bermuda, or some other place), which, of course, would be difficult to believe. She was living apparently in 1637: but it does not seem as if she went to New England at all. If Yonge's accusations are well founded, one could easily suppose that they lived apart. He married a second wife in 1639, another widow—by name Deliverance Sheffield.

When we come to accounts of Peters as a merchant and trader in the new colony, nothing can exceed the commendations of his chroniclers. They quite equal their approvals of his capacity as a teacher of religion or a political counsellor and as a framer and administrator of laws. "The father of our commerce, and the founder of our trade," is only one of the frequent expressions of esteem and favour lavished upon one whom Hume designated, in allusion to his later career, as "Cromwell's mad chaplain."* " While preaching at Boston and Salem," says one account, " he moved the country to raise a stock for fishing,† as the only probable means to free us from that oppression which the seamen and others held us under."

Peters was naturally a very busy man, in things secular as well as religious. Being frequently absent (from Salem), says his chronicler, " Mr. John Fiske "‡ (a name we have heard an echo of in modern times) "assisted him in his pulpit." Peters was a man of war, even in those early days. He had a considerable share in precipitating an attack on the Pequot Indians.

" Arriving at Fort Saybrook" (a name recalling those aristocratic members of the Massachusetts Bay Company, the Lords Say and Brooke) " with three other ministers or Councillors, it was in vain that Lyon Gardiner (Professor of Fortification, etc.) remonstrated against the ardour of these gentlemen."

* Palfrey, the American historian, pays Peters the following compliment : " He was a man of restless and various activity. He saw at once the commercial capacities of the country, and set himself to work to develop them " (" Palfrey's History," l., p. 436.)
† The figure of a codfish was suspended above the chair in the House of Assembly, perhaps at the suggestion of Hugh Peters.
‡ It is curious that Mr. Felt, the special biographer and admirer of Hugh Peters, omits all mention of Mr. Fiske as spiritual coadjutor, and only mentions Mr. Burdett and a Mr. Norris. And yet Fiske was a leading man apparently.

Alluding to Pequot captives after the conclusion of some fighting, Hugh Peters writes the following letter, which combines religion and business pleasantly and smartly:

"Sir,—Mr. Endicott and myself salute you in the Lord Jesus, etc. (*sic.*) We have heard of a divisioning of women and children in the Bay, and would be glad of a share, viz., a young woman or girl, and a boy if you think good. I wrote to you for some boys to Bermuda. . . . .
"HUGH PETERS."

These captives were used as slaves by the early colonists: later on they had negroes in New England also. The rooted objections of American girls to domestic service may possibly owe its origin to forced service required from natives.

Mr. Felt, in his account of Hugh Peters, has some *naive* remarks about a poor slave who served Peters, which are worth quoting: "With respect to his (Peters') domestic affairs, he had an Indian servant called Hope," probably one of the Pequot captives. "This person," continues Felt, "is brought to our notice in a way unfavourable to his character. A Court record informs us that for intemperance and running away he was sentenced to be whipped. The employment of such natives in families was anciently common in New England" ("Hugh Peters," Felt, p. 17). A footnote on this passage informs us that an " Indian of this name " (Hope), "a slave of Edward Winslow in Plymouth" (possibly Peters' unfortunate servant ?) was *sold* by an agent to John Mainford, of Barbadoes."

Thus did the New Englanders make a profit on most things, notwithstanding their excessive piety. In mentioning the fate of "Hope," whose "untutored mind" probably could not grasp Calvinistic tenets, we cannot help reflecting how he must have longed for the more "equal sky" which the poet talked of in his behalf.

Later on we read of a negro being sold in this colony, so that Massachusetts was not originally more spotless than colonies farther south in their dealings with blacks.

In later times Peters was not friendly to Indian " Missions. " In the " Hutchinson Papers " it is recorded that he opposed preaching to the Indians, though one of the Committee of the (Parliamentarian [?]) army for the advance of it."

A propos of this subject, a short passage from "Colonial State Papers" (Saintsbury, America and West Indies, 1661-8, p. 26) does not give us a very high opinion of Peters' probity. It is as follows: "Through the motion of Hugh Peters, England contributed nine hundred pounds per annum to Christianise the Indians of New England; which money found its way into private men's purses, and was a cheat of Hugh Peters."

This letter is annotated by Secretary Nicholas, the honest servant of Charles I.: "Concerning Mass. Bay, in N.E., and Hugh Peters' cheats."

Though Eliot's missionary labours may be boasted of, it ought to be remembered, to the credit of the much-abused Jesuits, that they alone, of all missionaries, were really successful in partly civilising the wild inhabitants of North America; facing all the terrible hardships and dangers consequent upon their enterprise "without the assistance of a mortal hand." This they did during the French occupation of Canada, in far-distant backwoods.

Both Vane and Peters were at one time in favour of severe laws. Finding "distractions" about the late Governor Dudley and the then

Governor Winthrop, they seem to have strongly sided with Dudley—a tyrannical archon, afterwards the deadly foe of Quakers.

The elder Winthrop was considered too mild, although by no means favouring the liberty of the subject, or as we should rather say, citizen. He, however, yielded to his more violent associates, promising "amendment by God's grace": the result being that Roger Williams, a sort of apostle of religious liberty, was, in the depth of winter, driven from the colony of Massachusetts for Nonconformity, to live as best he could in the wild forests of New England. He found the poor native savages more kind than his pious countrymen, and he accordingly availed himself of their hospitality, wretched though it must have been. He afterwards became the founder of Rhode Island Colony.

It was about this time, 1637, that a "Church Covenant," perhaps the precursor of the famous Scotch "Solemn League and Covenant," was invented. Peters' name stands third on the list of subscribers. Fiske, Peters' deputy at Salem, who preached a discourse on the occasion,* heads it. It appeared to have been signed by women as well as men.

* Though itself a copy of one got up by Hugh Peters in Holland.

Vane at this time, probably in consequence of his being the son and heir of the minister, Sir Harry Vane, was elected Governor, and Winthrop and Dudley were made Councillors for life. This last arrangement was supported by five texts from Holy Writ. Presently came the ferocious persecution of Ann Hutchinson, Peters at first being more moderate than the other tyrants. Soon afterwards, however, he changed his tone, and opposed Vane, who once more began to talk of that "liberty of conscience" of which he became in England later on a champion, though while sitting in the Governmental chair at Boston he did little to secure it.

In 1637 Peters severely blamed Vane to his face for his laxity of principle, saying that "it sadded the minister's spirits that he should seem to restrain *their* (!) liberties, and that he should consider his youth and inexperience in the things of God."

On this occasion it would seem that the afterwards formidable "Vane the Younger," the destroyer of Charles I.'s great minister, and one of the administrators of the Navy who sent Blake to sea, wept (!), and talked of resigning the Governorship of the Colony.

CHAPTER VIII.

Peters' Departure from New England.

Hugh Peters, afterwards to make such a figure in the Great Rebellion, left for the old country in 1641—according to one account, on a most appropriate day—the 3rd of September: a day afterwards noticed as Cromwell's day, sacred as it was to the memory of Drogheda's siege, Dunbar and Worcester fights, as well as the dramatic exit of the Usurper in a ferocious storm.

Peters left behind him his second wife, Deliverance (Sheffield), whom, as we mentioned, he had married in 1637. There is a letter which tends to show that for some time he could not make up his mind to marry her. She would seem to have been demonstrative in her regard for the popular minister. The objects of Peters in returning to England were twofold. One was commercial, the other political. He was to look after the interests of the Colony in the old country, and to explain to the discontented shareholders the present impossibility of paying them any dividend. Mr. Felt also observes that Peters, Weld, and Hibbins were "desired to inform the creditors of our merchants that a reason why they had delayed to forward payment of goods was the embarrassment of our trade."

His political object is best illustrated from American records. Governor Winthrop, June 2nd, 1641-2, writes:

"The Parliament of England sitting upon a general reformation of Church and State, and the Earl of Strafford being beheaded; and the Archbishop (Laud), our great enemy, and many others imprisoned and called to account—this caused men to stay in England in expectation of a new world . . . the General Court (*i.e.*, in Massachusetts) thought fit to send some chosen men to congratulate the happy success there, and to make use of any opportunity God should offer for the good of the Colony here, as also to give any advice as it should be required for the settling of the right form of Church discipline there. . . . The men chosen were HUGH PETERS, pastor of Salem; Mr. Thomas Weld, pastor of the Church in Roxburg; and Mr. William Hibbins, of Boston. They departed hence third of the sixth month, 1641 (o.s.) With them went J. Winthrop, Junr." *

Vane the Younger, afterwards apostrophised by Oliver in the famous words, "The Lord deliver me from Sir Harry Vane," had left some time previously with the young Lord Ley, son of the Earl of Marlborough. Just before they went they both refused to dine with Governor Winthrop, "for conscience' sake."

Ley appears to have been disgusted with all he saw in New England, and commented upon the treason against the King that he had constantly heard there.

The determination of the New Englanders to resist the King's government, is boasted of by Mr. Felt in his work (printed at Salem), giving a date subsequent to Ley's departure:

"April 12th, 1638. With the other churches, Peters' church at Salem solemnly keeps a fast day for Divine deliverance from the threatening evil of a general Government of the Colonies, and the consequent dissolution of their charter privileges, and the loss of all religious freedom,

* "Life and Letters of Winthrop," p. 297. J. Winthrop, Junr., married the step-daughter of Peters, *née* Read.

for which they had prayed, toiled, and suffered. This was (says Felt) emphatically a time of trial for Peters and the founders of the Commonwealth, who were in imminent peril of being brought under the power of the dominant party in England, from which they had fled. Sooner than give up their present liberties they felt themselves *sacredly bound to resist the forces** which they had expected would be sent over to impose upon them the dreaded yoke of hierarchy " (involving the Book of Common Prayer, surplice, altar-rails, etc.)

Probably in consequence of these warlike resolutions subsequent preparations were made to get munitions of war, apparently on credit. Mr. Felt records : " As he (Peters) was favourably known in Holland, the General Court requested him to send thither in their behalf for a supply of match and saltpetre—in another document described as " Salt *Peter* " (!)

The complaints which had come to the King of the contempt with which the extremely liberal charter was treated, had led to threats of Royal interference in behalf of the liberty of the subject. But the difficulties of government at home prevented any trouble being taken. And so the settlers did as they liked.

* Italics *not* in the original.

Mr. Felt mentions, without disapproval, the prohibition of the use of the Prayer Book (soon to be copied by English Reformers) in the following passage:

"Though a good degree of harmony prevailed among the inhabitants of Salem, yet it was not perfect. Messrs. Brown" (John and Samuel, mentioned before by Felt as having been well recommended by the company promoters at home) "contended for the Episcopal mode of worship. They had followers. They assembled by themselves on the Sabbath. They were reproved by the Governor and ministers as promoters of schism when strict union was so essential to the welfare of the Colony. They replied to their reprovers 'that *they* were Separatists, and would soon be Anabaptists; and, as for themselves, they would hold fast to the form of the Church established by law.' The Governor and ministers denied this, and stated they only came away from the Common Prayer and ceremonies because they judged the imposition of these things to be sinful corruptions of the Word of God. Such controversy increased warmth of feeling, and drove the subjects of it further from reconciliation, etc."

The historian Bancroft is much more frank and outspoken about the matter than Mr. J. B. Felt. "John and Samuel Brown," he says, "gathered a company in which the Common Prayer worship was upheld. . . . Both were members of the Colonial Council, and one of them an expert lawyer." Very soon, however, "they were seized like criminals" and "transported from Salem, because they were Churchmen" (!)*

Curious that in the Great Civil War between the Northern and Southern States another "John Brown" became a remarkable figure in story (and song)! History repeats itself—with variations.

It is as well to fortify the record left by Winthrop, about Peters' remarkable political mission and objects in crossing the Atlantic, by other quotations.

"Peters went to England," says another account, "upon the supposal that great revolutions were now at hand."†

Again, in "Sion's Saviours in New England," it is stated that "the Rev. Hugh Peters and his fellow-helper in Christ, Mr. Wells (*i.e.*,

* "Bancroft's History," I., 349-50.
† "Mass. Hist. Coll.," Second Series, VI., 371.

Weld), steered their course for England so soon as they heard of the chaining up of those biting beasts who went under the name of Spiritual Lords." Mr. Felt also observes: "On his trial Peters was represented as having told" (a witness) "that the main object of his visiting England was to advise the revolution and reformation. This statement," says Felt, "was probably an inference from the conversation in which it was predicated. True, it was in accordance with the wishes of himself, as well as of the authorities who sent him over, etc."

"Prior to Peters leaving New England," says Felt, "he had learned that the Parliament was set upon a general reformation. Bishop Laud, and the chief supporters of his policy, were imprisoned, and that, however, the Presbyterians, especially the Covenanters of Scotland, held great sway, . . . there was yet hope for Independency, and the opportunity for its advancement should be seasonably improved."

After he left Peters continued to trade with Salem; and in 1642 he had a stock of five hundred pounds on which he made eighty per cent. profit. He also settled the affairs of

Plymouth Colony as well as those of Massachusetts.

Yonge has, of course, no pity for the subject of his memoirs; but it does not follow that his account (though Mr. Gardiner, it is true, thinks so) should be entirely discredited.

"The classical clergy," says Yonge, meaning the ministers in New England, "finding Peters fitted for their design to stir up a commotion in England, give him his mission with their benediction. He was the patron of blasphemy, the prelate of rebellion, and mirror of all apostates and impostors . . . all the wit of London could not espie him till he had juggled their plate with their thimbles and bodkins into the Guildhall."

To England, then, we must go with Hugh Peters, to be a spectator and annotator of his melancholy career, rather corroborating than disproving the lamentable tale of William Yonge, M.D., which is somewhat confirmed even by Mr. Felt in his laudatory memoirs.

CHAPTER IX.

GODLY REFORMATION BEGUN.

THE memorable Long Parliament, which contained so many eminent men remarkable for deeds bad and good, had assembled on the 3rd November, 1640; and, by the time Hugh Peters arrived in London, had accomplished some wonderful things. "Those biting beasts," the Bishops, had been "chained up." Strafford had been impeached for high treason; tried; not found guilty, but voted so by Bill of Attainder; and beheaded on Tower Hill, marching to the place of execution more like a victorious Roman general celebrating his own triumph than as the "traitor" that his enemies vainly tried to make him out—the fox or wolf," as one of them compared him to—fit only "to be knocked on the head."

On the scaffold he told the people that "he feared the omen was bad for the intended reformation of the State, in that it commenced with the shedding of innocent blood."

Probably the paid rabble of London, which had been the material, though subordinate, agents in hounding him to death, swarmed on Tower Hill. But from the accounts we have, they and the rest of the hostile multitude must have been awed into silence by the majesty of the imperious, but great minded, ex-Lord Lieutenant of Ireland, who had governed the hitherto untamable people for seven years with notable success, and without bloodshed.

But the aspiring men who saw the grand and dreaded obstacle to their ambitious schemes removed, were contented with the prelude of victory. "What! hath he given us Strafford's head?" the exulting Pym had cried with uplifted hands; "then he will deny us nothing."

No doubt Pym, Hampden, St. John, and the rest remembered with grim satisfaction their vindictive promise about *not leaving* their former associate, *so long as his head was on his shoulders* (*!*)

The now appeased citizens, who had refused to open their shops till "justice had been done," went back to their work; while violent country partisans of progress, who had come up to London on sanguinary business, galloped home through towns and villages, shouting: "His head is off! his head is off!" What the astute Richelieu thought of the matter need not here be repeated. Nor do we propose here to join in the usual pastime of throwing mud upon the miserable, afflicted King for his share in the martyrdom of his minister. Far too much has already been thrown during the last seventy years.

We should like to know how many of Charles I.'s censorious critics would have acted otherwise than he did at that desperate and deplorable crisis. For Judges, Bishops, and Lords (except the partisans of progress) were all more or less smitten with fear. There was a reign of terror at Westminster and at Whitehall. The huge roaring armed mobs (managed by Venn, M.P., and the Rev. (!) Cornelius Burgess) which had overawed "the Straffordians" in both Houses by open violence, returned once more to Whitehall, to assist "King Pym" and his brethren in coercing King Charles to sign the warrant for Strafford's death. There were no "police" in those days; and the King's army, more or less tainted with disaffection and mutiny, was no nearer than York; and, therefore, no force was available to withstand the six thousand armed "roughs," to use a modern word.

The opportune discovery of the so-called "army plot" was, besides, favourable to democratic disorder.

While the dangerous ruffians before mentioned, shouting "Justice! Execution!" (" not without great and insolent threats and expressions of what they would do if it were not speedily granted,"*) swarmed round Whitehall, the King, who never much considered the question of his own personal safety, had good reason to apprehend what might happen to his Catholic wife, as well as to his children. Far from acting precipitately, however, he spent much time in anxious discussion. He got no support from his assembled Council. He summoned the Judges, who declared that what Strafford had done amounted to treason. The Bishops gave him no help—with the noble exception of Juxon—who, as is well known, advised the King not to act against his conscience. The Puritan Archbishop Williams, energetically pressing him to sign, talked about a twofold conscience; and some persons seem to have suggested that "it was better

* "Clarendon's History."

that one man should die than all the realm perish" (an argument worthy of Councillors at the Court of Benin!)

The general conclusion seemed to be that the King would perform a politic—and, in modern terms, a "constitutional"—act in surrendering Strafford (whom he probably had not actually the power to save) as a sacrifice to the GOD of the hour, namely, the foolishly incensed people, with the blood-thirsty party behind, who knew that their own safety was concerned if Strafford survived. For Strafford on the day of his impeachment had intended to impeach his impeachers.

That the tears of his wife, whom he so faithfully loved, were the chief arguments in persuading the King to comply with constitutional advisers, several historians have believed. *Cherchez la femme*, some will say, laying the blame on Henrietta Maria. But was not her alarm only too natural and reasonable? Alas! poor Queen, if it was her influence that prevailed, she herself suffered severely enough in after times!

The fatal moment which was to cause the King life-long remorse arrived. He signed the commission for four Lords to carry out the sentence, hoping even then, perhaps, that *certain promises of the triumphing party* might be made good. But there is something more not mentioned in most modern accounts to be told. With the same "full pen"—*i.e.*, without dipping it again in the ink—King Charles signed another Act placed before him, with still more fatal consequences to himself — namely, *the perpetuity of the Long Parliament*, which *henceforth was not to be dissolved, prorogued, or adjourned without its own consent!**

The "wicked Earl," as a merciless foe called him, was "stone dead"; his treason-plotting enemies were safe; and the sad, humiliated, and remorseful King was left to fight his battles alone! "Good-morrow, fellow-subject," a courtier is reported to have said, hailing the King with more freedom and humour than respect or sympathy on the morning after the fatal signature had been extorted; and the House of Commons set to work at a "godly thorough Reformation."

Men who afterwards went wholly over to the King, laboured persistently to destroy the pre-

* Mr. Gardiner—whose prejudices against Charles I. are probably as strong as those of Macaulay, Carlyle, and the late Mr. Bruce—deserves credit for his candour in allowing the existence of a terrorising mob at this crisis.

GODLY REFORMATION BEGUN 73

ponderating power of the Crown, inherited by the Stuarts from Elizabeth, Henry VIII., Henry VII., etc. The Star Chamber,* the Council of the North, the High Commission, the Court of Wards,† and several other engines of power, or sources of income, were swept away at a time when government was becoming difficult, or rather, as it proved, impossible. These changes were the direct consequences of Strafford's murder. The King's best friends helped, and some of them had also helped to doom Strafford— Falkland, Capell, and perhaps Hyde, amongst the number. Were they influenced by the pervading "fury of the people"? or were they following the dictates of conscience? We know certainly that one of the noblest and bravest of the King's friends voted the unjust sentence "*through fear.*" We have his own word for it on the scaffold. The self-accusing man was the heroic Capell, the betrayed prisoner of war, the undaunted defender of Colchester, and martyr in Palace

---

* The Star Chamber has had a bad name, and yet Lord Chancellor Bacon says "it subsisted by the common law of the realm, till confirmed in the time of Henry VII. by Act of Parliament, and was one of the wisest and noblest institutions of the kingdom . . . It took cognisance of violence, frauds, and all kinds of knavery, etc."

† Not completely abolished till just before the arrival of Charles II. at the Restoration.

Yard, six weeks after his Sovereign's decapitation. Let the unmerciful critics of King Charles's conduct ponder this fact at their leisure.

It is possible that in adding to the too great power of the now irremovable Parliament, Falkland and his associates thought they were but confirming the Great Charter, or creating a worthy imitation of the great republics of antiquity, which scholars and gentlemen were always inclined to venerate. It is quite likely that later on most of them secretly regretted the completeness of their work. Had they known what was coming, they would, perhaps, have endeavoured to postpone some of these sweeping changes to calmer moments and quieter times. The King naturally thought that things were going too fast, but he was powerless to oppose. He went to Scotland with the view, no doubt, of getting help from his native country, which he always favoured; but came back after putting his enemies there in power, and destroying his own without making anyone in any way grateful. These weak proceedings of the doomed King probably originated in his tenderness for his countrymen. For a moment, however, there seemed to some a possible end to the kingdom's difficulties. The King had surrendered so much that it might well be supposed that the "violent party," as Clarendon calls them, would be satisfied. That party, however, had ulterior designs far-reaching in character. "Religion" had to be settled according to their notions, and a "root-and-branch" reform of the Church could not be carried out in a day. Although "those biting beasts," the Bishops, had been "chained up," the punishment of the aged Archbishop of Canterbury, suggested in some remarkable lines in "Lycidas," had yet to be arranged. The "militia" also, *i.e.*, the armed forces of the kingdom by sea and land, had yet to be put into safe (!) hands. Suddenly, while the King was in Scotland, came the news of the Irish massacre, which began on October 23rd, 1641. On the preceding 12th of May the strong hand, which for seven years had ruled the Land of Ire, as Fuller called it, with eminent success, had been for ever relaxed. A little more than five months had passed, and the consequences were plain to all who were not following a will-o'-the-wisp. To strong settled government anarchy had succeeded.

* According to Prendergast and others not the wholesale act of slaughter by some believed in.

The King proposes to raise a large force of volunteers, and to go to Ireland in person with them to put down rebellion there. But he cannot be trusted by his loyal, or rather politic subjects at Westminster. The Parliament will settle matters for him, but they must first have the control of the "militia" entirely in their own hands. And there are peculiar religious complications. The truth is that the massacre of Irish Protestants was a bagatelle compared with other things that were in hand. No sooner did the King, who was already shorn of most of his power, return to Whitehall, than they presented him with their GRAND REMONSTRANCE.

CHAPTER X.

Peters and the Great Rebellion.

The assembly of divines at Westminster had not yet begun to sit in Henry VII.'s chapel and make an end of the Book of Common Prayer, Episcopacy, etc., and complete the godly, thorough Reformation. Hugh Peters took a strong line about the constitution of that assembly. Spiritual representatives were wanted from New England; but Peters disapproved, so they were not sent. Possibly Peters thought that his advice would be quite sufficient; and, indeed, Peters, Weld, and Hibbins *were spiritual delegates from New England, with plenary powers.*

Not long after his arrival in England, Peters, according to his own account, was employed as a paid "lecturer" in the City. Perhaps, after a short career there, he "joined the Scottish interest," as Yonge says, "and goes to Ireland (? 1641), commanding a brigade," at what exact date we have not ascertained.* Whitelock (who, no doubt, was obliged to speak no ill of Peters, seeing he was patronised by Cromwell) speaks favourably of Peters' "military" service there. And Felt is still more complimentary. What actual exploits he performed against the marauding Irish rebels seems not defined. Yonge does not think much of him as a fighting man. True, Yonge did not know him till eight years later, when Peters had supped full of horrors, and, besides the wars in England, had seen, and to a certain extent shared in, the Drogheda and Wexford hecatombs. It is, at all events, likely he was not behindhand in sounding his own trumpet on his return to England, though there may be some slight exaggeration in Yonge's description of his bringing back "a packet of lies" about his exploits and sufferings in Ireland.

On his arrival from New England Peters had interviewed the King on Colonial business. He got, he says, a "civil reception." After his Irish trip, Peters goes on a diplomatic mission

* "My first work," says Peters, "was for Ireland, where I had many hazards." He adds: "Then I was at sea with my old patron, the Earl of Warwick, *to whom I owed my life.*" He says he went into Ireland "with Lord Forbes."

to Holland, in behalf of New England. And it must not be forgotten that part of his duty was to explain to grumblers how it was they were not to expect any money at present. He, however, also preached sermons in behalf of the Irish Protestants who had suffered in the recent massacre.

Whatever his previous conduct may have been in Holland, we may be sure that the "godly" party there must now have looked on him as a distinguished, successful, and important personage ; an active man of business, as well as a shining light from the free land of the West, where the millenium was already begun, and the enemies of the Lord nowhere to be found—now that the Browns and the Prayer Book were banished—except incipient Quakers, such as Roger Williams and Ann Hutchinson.

So powerful was his preaching at Rotterdam, and perhaps in other places, and so great the impression he made upon the female part of his congregations, that women are reported to have contributed their wedding rings for the benefit of the sufferers in Ireland. Hugh Peters, already the mortal enemy of King Charles, owed this grand success chiefly to false statements of the great share which

Charles and Henrietta Maria had in stirring up the Irish to deeds of blood against the friends of the godly Parliament party.

Ludlow—perhaps, however, mainly on the authority of Peters—says that Peters collected in Holland no less than thirty thousand pounds. There may possibly be some corroboration; but the sum seems large, and looks like an instance of Peters' spread-eagleism.*

It is not necessary here to repeat the tale of the attempted arrest of the FIVE MEMBERS, nor to discuss the share that the Lady Carlisle had in its being foiled. Neither shall we go into the matter of the King's final departure from Whitehall and retreat to York. Contrary to the expectation of his enemies, the King at last made a decided stand, and absolutely (after much discussion) refused to surrender the command of the armed forces of the kingdom to the Parliament. By the fundamental laws of the land—notwithstanding Pym's attempt to prove the contrary—it was, no doubt, his duty to refuse.

Thereupon the Parliament seizes Hull and the Tower, the dockyards and arsenals, Dept-

---

* Mr. Firth seems not to believe this story, or, at least, has not, we think, mentioned it.

ford, Woolwich, and Chatham; and later on possessed themselves of Portsmouth. They also voted their illegal ordinance for the militia, with the view of fighting against the apparently checkmated King in his own name! The command of the army and the command of the navy were given to great Lords hostile to the King's interests.

The subterfuge of " King and Parliament," as an authority for these outrageously illegal acts, deserves credit for what our transatlantic cousins would characterise as a "smart" invention. Poor innocent provincials (at a time when "the Press" had not been invented) as well as the seamen generally, were, no doubt, in large numbers deluded by it. Of course, it could not well deceive instructed gentlemen, who now began seriously to take sides. Although the King's friends did not at once take up arms, Clarendon gives us an example of the view which a Royalist member of the Long Parliament took at this crisis. "The members of both Houses," says he, after quoting the Parliamentarian propositions of the 10th of June, 1642, for raising an army to fight against the King, who as yet had not even a guard for his person, "appointed a solemn day to set down their own subscriptions, which they performed liberally."

"Most of those," Clarendon continues, "who abhorred their impious designs, not thinking it lawful for them to be present at such consultations, withdrew before the day came or absented themselves thence. But many had the courage to be present. . . . Sir Henry Killigrew, who was notoriously an enemy to all these devices, being called upon, told them "if there were occasion, he would provide a good horse and a good sword; and made no question that he should find a good cause."

It was not long before he made good his promise.

At length the King, reduced apparently to a cipher and virtually dethroned—the Parliament having usurped his authority, seized his revenues, and the command and control of his armed forces by sea and land—determined to bring matters to a crisis by testing the strength of treasonable resolutions. He demands entrance with a small following into his town of Hull; and, being refused by the Governor Hotham on the walls—in what we might call "a form of prayer" (for Hotham fell on his knees)—withdrew; and, after long and fruitless correspondence with his determined enemies, on the 25th (?) August, 1642,* in order to get help from the loyal part of the nation, raised his standard at Nottingham.

Momentous decision, but absolutely necessary under the circumstances. It is very certain that his enemies believed at this time that the King was so unpopular that there was no chance of his getting any considerable following. In this they were very much mistaken.

Now was a busy time in the City of London for Parliamentarian preachers.

To get a true idea of these individuals it is not amiss again to quote Clarendon—a writer not sufficiently valued at the present day—the justness of whose portraits of the men of his time, as also his accounts of the great events in which he was a prominent actor, were allowed by the age succeeding, as also by the most eminent in recent times, to rival in merit the efforts of the greatest of historical pens, whether ancient or modern. His judgment of men, indeed, was evidently so acute, that it is somewhat surprising that modern historians

---

* According to Lilly, the astrologer, who drew out a horoscope, the 22nd of August was the day.

should so frequently dare not only to qualify, but to reverse his descriptions and criticisms.

"I must not forget," says our English Tacitus, "though it cannot be remembered without horror, that this strange wild-fire among the people was not so much and so furiously kindled by the breath of Parliament as of the clergy, who both administered fuel and blew the coals in the Houses too. These men having crept into, and at last driven all learned and orthodox men from the pulpits, had . . . from the beginning of this Parliament, under the notion of reformation and extirpating of Popery, infused seditious inclinations into the hearts of men against the present government of the Church, with many libellous invectives against the State too. But since the raising of an army, and rejecting the King's last overture of a treaty, they contained themselves within no bounds ; and as freely and without control inveighed against the person of the King as they had before against the worst 'malignant'; profanely and blasphemously applying whatsoever had been spoken by God Himself, or the prophets, against the most wicked and impious kings, to incense and stir up people against their most gracious Sovereign.

"There are monuments enough in the seditious sermons at that time printed,* and, in the memories of men, of others not printed, of such wresting and perverting of Scripture to the odious purposes of the preacher, that pious men will not look over without trembling.

"One takes his text out of Moses' words in the thirty-second chapter of Exodus and the twenty-ninth verse: 'Consecrate yourselves to-day to the Lord, even every man upon his son, and upon his brother; that He may bestow upon you a blessing this day'; and from thence incites his auditory to the utmost prosecution of those under what relation soever of blood, neighbourhood, dependence, who concurred not in the reformation proposed by the Parliament.

"Another makes us bold with David's words in the First Book of Chronicles, twenty-second chapter, verse sixteen, 'Arouse, therefore, and be doing'; and from thence assures them it was not enough to wish well to the Parliament, if they brought not their purse as well as their prayers, and their hands as well as their hearts to the assisting of it, the duty in the text was not performed.

* Still to be found in that wonderful collection called "The King's Pamphlets," given by George III. to the British Museum.

"There was more than Mr. Marshall, who from the twenty-third verse of the fifth chapter of Judges: 'Curse ye Meroz, said the Angel of the Lord; curse ye bitterly the inhabitants thereof: because they came not to the help of the Lord against the mighty'; presumed to inveigh against, and in plain terms to pronounce God's own curse against, all those who came not with their utmost power and strength to destroy and root out all the malignants who in any degree opposed the Parliament.

"There was one who, from the forty-eighth chapter of the Prophet Jeremiah and the tenth verse, 'Cursed be he that keepeth back his sword from blood,' reproved those who gave any quarter to the King's soldiers; and another, out of the fifth verse of the twenty-fifth chapter of Proverbs, 'Take away the wicked from before the King, and his throne shall be established in righteousness,' made it no less a case of conscience by force to remove the evil councillors from the King (with bold intimation what might be done to the King himself if he would not suffer them to be removed) than to perform any Christian duty that is enjoined. It would fill a volume to insert all the impious madness of this kind, so that the complaint of the Prophet Ezekiel might most truly and reasonably have been applied: 'There is a conspiracy of her prophets in the midst thereof like a roaring lion ravening the prey; they have devoured souls; they have taken the treasures and precious things; they have made her many widows in the midst thereof. . . .' And, indeed, no good Christian can, without horror, think of those members of the Church who, by their function being messengers of peace, were the only trumpets of war and incendiaries of rebellion. How much more Christian was that Athenian nun in Plutarch, and how shall she rise up in judgment against those men, who, when Alcibiades was condemned by the public justice of the State, and a decree made that all the religious priests and women should ban and curse him—stoutly refused to perform that office, answering 'that she was professed religious to *pray* and to *bless*, not to *curse* and to *ban*.' And if the person and the place can improve and aggravate the offence (as without doubt it doth, both before God and man), methinks the preaching treason and rebellion out of the pulpit should be worse than the advancing it in the market, as much as poisoning a man at the communion would be worse than murdering him at a tavern," etc.

Can we doubt that the busy, active, and meddling Peters, chief apostle from the God-fearing American plantations, was less zealous than Burgess, or Calamy, or Marshal? or any of the reverend persons whose initials made up the word " Smectymnus," who sent forth the " thimble and bodkin " army, as it was called, to fight King Charles at Edgehill?

One Parliamentarian assurance no doubt aided Peters and his colleagues in the good work; namely, that the pious contributors were to receive eight per cent for their offerings.†

The investment proved to be utterly bad. That eight per cent., neither on " thimbles and bodkins," which poor women subscribed, nor on the more valuable contributions of wealthy Saints, was ever paid. The Grand Committees of London, no less than the County Commit-

---

* " Clarendon's History," III., 230-3. The concluding lines of this extract, though, of course, not specially directed against Hugh Peters, condemn him absolutely.

† On the 10th of June, 1642, the Parliament published their propositions for raising an army in the King's name to fight against the King. " And they further declare," says Clarendon (Vol. III., p. 62), " that whosoever brought in money or plate, or found or maintained horsemen or arms, upon their propositions should be repaid their money at eight per cent."

tees which fleeced the Royalists, were always in want of money, though thousands upon thousands passed through their hands. Leading Saints, however, got far more than eight per cent. from public plunder. We may reasonably conclude that the piously jocular Peters—who, when after one hour's sermon had come to an end, he turned the sand—would remark: "What do you say, beloved, to another glass?" (meaning another sermon one hour in length) occasionally enlivened his dreary religious treason with jokes neither too reverential nor too refined.

Yonge, M.D., thus severely describes the pulpit career of Peters:

"He composes three canons to walk by.

"To admire the gentry.

"To delude and blind the commonalty.

"To excite and cherish the soldiery, which last he told that they earned martyrdom, and carried Jesus Christ in their knapsacks.

"Two obstructions were in Peters' way," observes Yonge. "The Book of Common Prayer and the Bishops. *Divide et impera* was his Gospel rule until he had brought all into confusion."

A sad description indeed, and not easy to disprove, though it will have been seen by what Clarendon says that Peters was not the only pulpit firebrand and war trumpeter of that lamentable time.

CHAPTER XI.

MILTON AND PETERS.

DID Milton know Peters before the latter commenced his career as army chaplain? Can we doubt it, when we remember what a position Peters occupied in founding the Massachusetts Bay Company? How the Lords Warwick, Brooke, and Say, not to mention other pre-eminent Puritans, were mixed up in that commercial and supposed freedom-promoting association, there are sufficient hints. We have mentioned how Peters took upon himself to rebuke the freely elected Governor of the Colony, "Vane the Younger," and how that Governor thereupon shed tears.

It is pretty certain that Milton must have watched with interest the developments of civil freedom and "purity of doctrine and worship" there. But he seems to have thought more of the hardships the emigrants had suffered than of the supreme spiritual advantages they had secured. In his thundering discourse on "Reformation in England," written probably just after his return from Italy, before the Long Parliament had been summoned, he exclaims :

"What numbers of faithful and free-born Englishmen and good Christians have been constrained to forsake their dearest home, their friends and kindred, when nothing but the wide ocean and the savage deserts of America could hide or shelter from the fury of the Bishops?" And he continues his pathetic lament, not considering, however, what he probably knew— that a spiritual tyranny far more severe than that of the Bishops had almost immediately sprung up in New England, and that a man, merely for accusing Peters, and Dudley, and other "godly" persons in high place of being "under a covenant of works," was driven into the savage wilds of the American forests, in the depth of winter, to live upon the charity of savages ; and that non-conforming women were even worse treated by these Gospel Saints and Republicans.

All the shining lights of that time, including Fieunes, Say, Brooke, Hampden, and Cromwell, were certainly not ignorant of what was going on under the ægis of the violated Massachusetts charter before Peters arrived in England. But after the advent of that express agent and apostle of New England Saintship, the lively, active, and garrulous missionary from Salem would not long leave them uninformed. It is impossible not to believe that there was an active private correspondence kept up—as far as distance would permit—between the Scotch and other would-be Covenanters and the New England Council.

The Scottish Covenant was possibly the outcome of the obscure " Church Covenant," adopted at Salem and signed by Peters and his coadjutor Fiske, although the Salem Covenant did not mention as a leading motive " the protection of the King's person "—which person, indeed, the Saints of New England completely ignored, and even attempted to reject, when Governor Endicott cut the cross out of the English flag.

One of the most portentous agencies in the approaching bloody and destructive cataclysm in England was the trumpet of John Milton. That of Peters, though it sounded loudly and mischievously, was only a vulgar echo.

It is sad to think what the writer of " l'Allegro" and "Il Penseroso" became. The "loathed melancholy" which he exorcised in 1634 returned from its "Stygian cave" in 1639 to perplex and darken his fancy, and to seize and hold him in twenty-one years' forced servitude against the persons as well as against the offices of the King and the Bishop—against the State and against the Church.

He did not actually flourish a visible sword, like Hugh Peters; but no poisoned weapon was ever more fatal and deadly than the pen of the inspired poet, who invented the sad political word MALIGNANT;* and who, after twenty-one years, found that all his fiery paragraphs had been futile. His free republic, as well as the government of a single person without Lords and Commons, had vanished; the King and the Bishop returned, and the Latin Secretary to "His Highness" found himself "wanted," as was also *pseudo*

---

* Strange to say, this fact escaped the notice of Samuel Johnson, who in his dictionary only quotes it as used by Butler, in "Hudibras." See, however, Milton's "Reason of Church Government," etc., concluding page, where he thunders a concluding curse against "Prelaty" (*sic*). He also employed the word "blooming" in a way which to modern eyes and ears recalls Rudyard Kipling. See "Defence of the English People," apostrophe to Cromwellian "grandees." "O! Fleetwood, whom I have known from a boy to the present *blooming* maturity of your military fame" (!) The word "malignant" is also to be found in the "Grand Remonstrance."

St. Peter, whom Milton had, perhaps unwittingly, helped into the vacant chair of the murdered Archbishop Laud. We say "unwittingly," for it appears certain that Milton had but a poor opinion of Peters.

In studying that well-known menacing passage in "Lycidas":

> But that two-handed engine at the door
> Stands ready to smite once, and smite no more :

(the clean cut of the headsman!) One cannot avoid the suspicion that Milton had some private personal reason for hating with immortal hatred the foredoomed Archbishop. It does not seem quite certain, notwithstanding indignant denials, that something had occurred at Cambridge which had entailed censure, if not punishment,* upon the heaven-born genius, but supremely independent student. It was probably the promulgation of the Scottish Covenant† which brought back Milton in hot haste from Italy in 1639. It is quite a mistake to suppose that actual civil war brought him back, for it had not commenced. But he pro-

---

* The legend that Milton was whipped by William Chappell (afterwards Provost of Trinity College, Dublin), the friend of Strafford, may here be remembered.

† Significantly mentioned in 1639 by Sir Henry Wotton, the friendly patron of Milton (see "Relig. Wott.") "The Scottish Covenanters say they will have none but Christ to reign over them : *a serious cover for the deepest impiety*" (!)

bably perceived that there was now some prospect of violently reforming away the Bishops. If he was not actually invited by some of the future managers of rebellion, he was conscious of the power of his pen. It is thus he apologises for not drawing his sword like some other men of strong Republican principles: "I did not," says he at a later period, "for any other reason decline the toils and dangers of war, than that I might in another way, with much more efficacy and with not less danger to myself, render assistance to my countrymen," etc.

Considering the ferocious feeling against Laud, which began to culminate in his impeachment for high treason and imprisonment in the Tower, shortly following the deadly attack upon Strafford in 1640, it seems not improbable that if any of the "root and branch" party had any literary taste they might have committed to memory (some time before) the sanguinary passage in "Lycidas" already quoted. And not only that, but might have already determined that the motto "Stone-dead hath no fellow" would serve for dealing with Canterbury as with his ally the Lord Lieutenant of Ireland. Later on, the recorded gloomy remark of Cromwell to Falkland about his intention of selling all he had and (?) going to New England with other irreconcilable enemies of Church and King—if the "Grand Remonstrance" had not been carried—seems to point again to the material destruction of Episcopacy and its head.

Doubtless Peters, Marshal, Calamy, Dell, and Cornelius Burgess, as well as other vehement preachers of sedition, were unceasing in advocating "condign punishment" as a final step towards Gospel Reformation. But, as we said before, the voice of Milton (through his pen) sounds the highest leading note.

Sometimes it is the rude tone of the coarse jester. Sometimes it sounds like the voice of an angel; but as frequently it is like nothing else but the hoarse hellish trumpet of the Italian poet :*

> Chiama gli abitator' dell' ombre cterne,
> Il rauco suon della Tartarea trombá
> Treman le spaziose Atre Caverne
> E l'air 'cieco a quel rumor rimbomba!

Hear him before the war of actual rebellion—indeed, two years before—when the alliance between some future Parliamentarian leaders with Scotch Covenanters was being cemented. Listen to the refined flattery to the Covenant-

* Tasso.

ing party which he pretends has the entire sympathy of the two nations; but makes us rather think of Harmodius and Aristogeiton :

"Go on hand in hand, O nations never to be disunited. Be the praise and the heroic song of all posterity (!) Merit this, but seek only virtue ; not to extend your limits (for what need you wear a fading triumphant laurel out of the tears of wretched men?), but to settle the pure worship of God in His Church and justice in the State. Then shall the hardest difficulties smooth themselves before you : envy shall sink to hell : craft and malice shall be confounded, whether it be home-bred mischief or outlandish enemies. Yea, other nations will then court to serve you, for lordship and victory are but her two run-a-gates. Join your invincible might to do worthy and god-like deeds ; and then he who seeks to break your union—a *cleaving* curse be his inheritance to all generations."

In varied strain he goes on till we come to the following :—

". . . Seeing, therefore, the perilous and confined state in which we are fallen, and that to the certain knowledge of all men through the religious pride and hateful tyranny of prelates (as the innumerable and grievous complaints of every shire cry out), if we will now resolve to settle affairs, either according to pure religion or sound policy, we must first begin roundly to cashier and *cut away* from the public body the noisome and diseased tumour of prelacy, and come from schism to unity with our neighbour reformed sister churches, which, with the blessing of peace and pure doctrine, have now long time flourished, etc."

After a bitter impeachment of Episcopacy and its attendant corruptions and evils, he by-and-bye shows that Reformation ought to be sudden, and could not be so dangerous as some think :

"Speedy and vehement," says he, "were the reformations of all the good Kings of Judah" (here is the grand Puritan idea of fighting and governing after the pattern of the Old Testament), "though the people had been muzzled in idolatry ever so long before. They feared not the bugbear danger, nor the lion in the way that the sluggish and timorous politician thinks he sees ; no more did our brethren of the reformed churches abroad ; they ventured (God being their guide) out of rigid Popery into what we call in mockery 'precise Puritanism,' and yet we see no inconvenience befell them. . . ."

And, in fine, after almost inspired prayers and wonderful predictions of the blessed state in which England shall find herself when the Geneva discipline is fully established, he ends with a description of the prizes which will accrue in realms above to faithful partisans—thrones, principalities, and hands clasped in ecstatic bliss. He concludes with a picture of what will happen to those who care to flourish under the old *régime*.

"*But they contrary*," says he (meaning the opposers of his ideal religious republic, plainly all who are Churchmen and Royalists)—" But they contrary, that by the impairing and diminution of the true faith, the distress and servitude of their country aspire to high dignity, rule, and promotion here ; after a shameful end in this life (which God grant them) (!) shall be thrown down eternally into the darkest and deepest gulf of hell, where, under the despiteful control, the trample, and spurn of all the other damned, that in the anguish of their torture shall have no other ease than to exercise a raving and bestial tyranny over them as their slaves and negroes, they shall remain in that plight for ever—the basest, the lowermost, the most dejected, most underfoot and down-trodden vassals of perdition" (!)

* * * * * *

Here we may perceive foreshadowings of scenes in "Paradise Lost" confusedly mingled with terrific visions from Dante's "Inferno." The *Tartarea Tromba* with a vengeance! Curses louder, deeper, and far more dreadful than those which Cicero poured upon the would-be reckless destroyer of Old Rome, "*Hisce ominibus Catalina. . . vivos mortuosque mactabis!*"*

Sufficiently terrible if John Milton were only composing a drama, and giving vent to strong language recited from a puppet's mouth. But these words were really and earnestly and savagely meant! Mad zealot, imagining that the great God of the universe was wholly on his side!

What wonder, after this, when a mighty VATES (for are not prophet and poet synonymous?) expresses such fiendish and ungoverned rage against things that such men as Richard Hooker, to say nothing of millions of other excellent men, had venerated—what wonder,

* Oration against Cataline.

we say, if after such an example, not only that the coming Long Parliament (or the angry portion of it) should wage an illegal and relentless war against the King (and the Church) they had sworn to honour and protect. Not only that, but that Harrison, Ireton, and Cromwell, and hordes of more or less ruthless Independents (true precursors of modern dynamitards, as Sir Henry Maine proclaims[*]), should go forth with mad enthusiasm; or cold, bloodthirsty purpose, to kill, slay, and destroy; to plunder and desecrate, cathedrals and churches; to beat down, sack, and burn the castles and houses of loyal gentlemen true to their oaths; to hunt to destruction thousands of pious, honourable, and learned clergymen, as if they had been foxes or hares; now breaking faith with prisoners "rendered to mercy" (as in the case of Lisle, Lucas, and Capell, and hundreds of poor, common soldiers, after Colchester); now making quarter a byword, in order to put the whole of a brave Royalist garrison to the sword, and also to burn some of them to death (as at Drogheda,[†] shortly after which

[*] See "Popular Government."
[†] "Drogheda quarter" was the sarcastic phrase in use, both amongst Catholics and Protestants, after that inhuman business.

solemn thanks were given to God Almighty, in the Dublin Cathedral, "for this great mercy" (!) amidst the hum of the levelling army applauding the blasphemous words of Hugh Peters, "Minister of God's Word and Chaplain to the Lord Lieutenant ").

O, great John Milton! divine poet, but sad Roundhead — why did you not leave the task of stirring up all this devilish mischief to common treason trumpeters? For indeed there was stricter and sterner goverment, much more inconvenient to the subject, under the revered Elizabeth than under Charles—no matter what her flatterers have said—heavier punishments for rebels, severer sentences in the Star Chamber. How much better and pleasanter would it have been for you and for us, if you had never forsaken your innocent youthful Muse at Horton, in sight of the "towered battlements" of Windsor Castle, "bosomed high in tufted trees." When you invoked "heart-easing Mirth," and wished to be admitted of her "crew," to live not in Puritan preciseness, but in "unreproved pleasures free":

> To hear the lark begin his flight
> And singing startle the dull night
> From his watch-tow'r in the skies
> Till the dappled dawn doth rise;

> Then to come in spite of sorrow
> And at my window bid good morrow,
> Through the sweet-briar and the vine,
> Or the twisted eglantine.
>
> * * * *
>
> Sometimes walking, not unseen,
> By hedge-row elms on hillocks green,
> Right against the eastern gate,
> Where the great sun begins his state,
> Robed in flames of amber light,
> The clouds in thousand liveries dight.

When you sang in this strain, whether of the pastimes of town or country, in those matchless poems of your golden days—how happy you must have been!

Not far off was your refined friend, the Provost of Eton, and your learned friend, the "ever memorable" John Hales, the discoverer of Shakespearian literary merit,* who did not turn rebel and pugnacious Saint—having some time previously "bid" cruel "John Calvin good night!"

All reasonable men must feel sorry for you, John Milton; and regret that you thought it your solemn duty to assist (sometimes as the paid scribe) in the Pandemonium of Rebellion.

* *N.B.*—Not long before the Great Rebellion began.

CHAPTER XII.

PETERS AND THE FIRST WAR.

AFTER the war actually began, in 1642, Peters, by his old patron and associate in Colonial ventures, the Lord Brooke, was given the appointment to his own regiment of chaplain. So Peters' military career, partly initiated in wars against the Pequot Indians in N.E., is resumed. He must soon, of course, have been well known to the Earl of Essex, though we have not discovered what Essex thought of him, except as regards his behaviour to Laud. Possibly he may have considered him an unavoidable ally. After the fall of Essex, consequent 'upon the ill success at Lostwithiel, and the triumph of the grand Independent plot—Peters attached himself to the new great Presbyterian commander of the Reformed Army, Sir Thomas Fairfax — who, indeed, seems to have made him chaplain to six regiments. His ultimate appointment was "chaplain to the train." Considering that Peters was getting very considerable profits from "the Bay," as a shareholder in the Company, he must have been fairly well off at the beginning of his military career. There were besides stray crumbs to be picked up. "He became," says the sarcastic Yonge, "the post-priest as well as the divinity jester at Whitehall and the Council Boards. Only Mr. Peters his news were regarded as oracles. Witness the many fifty pounds, given him for postage, which made him often aver he would rather be supplanting in Old England than planting in the New!"

In illustration and partial support of Yonge's remarks, we may state that Peters was often sent by Fairfax and Cromwell to announce a victory *viva voce* to the House of Commons, though sometimes he communicated by letter only.

Among these announcements were those of the army triumphs at Lyme, Bridgewater, the taking of Bristol, of Winchester Castle, of Dartmouth, of the sack of Basing House—the massacre of Ormond's officers and soldiers—all recorded by Whitelock, and generally by Rushworth. Some few of these messages we shall presently allude to in detail. Peters got a hundred pounds for bringing to the House of Commons the news of the success at Bridgewater; and fifty pounds for bringing Cromwell's letters about the taking of Winchester Castle. Probably he was equally well paid on other occasions. Possibly this popular war trumpeter made money also by printing and selling letters and sermons. When Laud was tried Peters naturally appears upon the scene.

CHAPTER XIII.

PETERS AND LAUD.

AT Archbishop Laud's trial Peters was probably present. At all events, we have the poor Archbishop's actual authority that he was there at the commencement, Laud having made a speech before the House of Lords explaining how he had converted a good many Roman Catholics.

" I was commanded," says he " to withdraw. . . . I went into the little committee chamber at the entering of the House. There Mr. Peters followed me in great haste, and began to give me ill language, and told me that he and other ministers were able to name thousands they had converted. I knew him not, as never having seen him to my remembrance in my life; though I had heard enough of him. And, as I was going to answer him, one of my counsel, Mr. Hearn, seeing how violently he began, stept between us, and told him of his uncivil carriage towards me in my affliction; and, indeed, he came as if he would have struck me. By this time some occasion brought the Earl of Essex into the room, and Mr. Hearn complained to him of Mr. Peters' usage to me, who very honourably checked him for it, and sent him forth."*

We may here remark that the Earl of Essex was still Peters' commanding officer; but was on the point of being superseded by the "self-denying ordinance" and "new model," by Fairfax.

Later on, when sentence of death had been passed, Hugh Peters visited Laud in prison, with the design of getting him to consent to be sent to New England (Bishop Wren was to go too) instead of being decapitated.

It is not difficult to believe that the alternative of the scaffold was less terrible to the aged and infirm prelate than the prospect of being transported across the roaring Atlantic to the wild New England shore, in the depth of a nearly Arctic winter, to enjoy the company and counsels of vindictive Saints.† He might well

---

* " State Trials."

† " The plot was laid," says Laud, " by Peters and others of that crew, that they might insult over me."

at that time recall a passage from Scripture concerning some peculiar kinds of "tender mercies."*

Besides haranguing the Parliamentarian soldiers as a prelude to assaults upon His sacred Majesty's armies or garrisons, Peters was naturally ready to prepare culprits for death.

Clarendon, who perhaps knew what he was writing about, gives a very damaging account —which, of course, the defenders of Hugh Peters entirely disagree with — of what happened at the execution of the Hothams, the elder of whom, as Governor of Hull for the Parliament, had refused to admit the King, thus becoming the actual cause of the King's raising his standard at Nottingham. As is well known, the two Hothams suffered two

* A peculiarly suggestive passage occurs in Peters' prefatory remarks to a long pamphlet called "Church Government and Church Covenant" (a reply to English ministers by New England elders to thirty-two questions sent over in 1640). In the year 1643 Peters, recommending the pamphlet, says: "I do conceive that this sword will not be sheathed which is now drawn, till Church work is better known. Presbytery and Independency are the ways of Church fellowship now looked at, *since we hope Episcopacy is coffined out, and will be buried without expectation of another resurrection (!)*

N.B.—Laud was buried at All Hallow's, Barking, January 4th, 1644 (O.S.). On that very day (*vide* Rushworth) came out "An Ordinance for abolishing the Book of Common Prayer and establishing the Directory."

years later for treason against the Parliament. Clarendon's expression of "ungodly confessor," as applied to Peters, is naturally censured as "untrue." Peters also "confessed" Challoner. Did he share in the pious persecution of the dying Chillingworth, mentioned severely by Clarendon, who, however, neither mentions Peters nor the detestable Cheynell?

CHAPTER XIV.

Peters maligns King Charles.

AFTER the new model was established (1645) "Peters," says Yonge, "deserted Fairfax for Cromwell," though Fairfax had made him chaplain to six regiments. He became very intimate with the future Lord Protector, and was "Cromwell's Privy Councillor." Whitelock confirms Yonge in this statement amongst many others.

After the splendid Castle of Raglan had fallen, bravely defended through the long siege by the old Catholic Marquis of Worcester, who had lived there long years in regal state, Cromwell seems to have got something like eighteen thousand pounds or twenty thousand pounds per annum out of Lord Worcester's lands, and Peters about one thousand pounds per annum (modern computation).* Peters also got at least about

* Four thousand, says Clement Walker, equal now probably to about five times that amount. It was well said by the elder Disraeli that "The 'History of Independence' contained 'the secret political history of the time.'"

one thousand pounds per annum out of Lord Craven's* sequestered property, so that he was not neglected by Parliament or party friends, and must have been an important "object lesson" to other pious ministers of the Gospel. "Give God all the praise!" was the usual fervent ejaculation, either when confiscations were considerable in amount, or Royalists in large numbers were put to the sword.†

The fatal Battle of Naseby, where the King's forces, as at the second Battle of Newbury, were vastly inferior to those of his opponents, destroyed the chances of Royalist success; and when the year 1646 (o.s.) began, all hope of fighting at that time came to an end, and the King was obliged to depart secretly from Oxford, and seek an asylum with the Scotch army, which resulted in his being sold to the English Parliament.

Peters—who was with Fairfax in the West

* This Craven was, later on, the gallant commander of the King's Guard, who at eighty years of age would have defended James II., at Whitehall, against William III., to the death, if he had not been peremptorily ordered by James to desist.

† Peters at a later period affirmed that his good pay was not of much value, as he was obliged to share his wealth with others. No doubt, being looked on as the successor of the Archbishop of Canterbury, he was obliged to show hospitality to the "godly" ministry.

when he was finishing triumphant operations, assisted by Cromwell, with his well-paid and well-equipped army there—had preached a strong anti-Royalist sermon, after the capture of the town, in the market-place of Torrington.

But it was now time for him to think of deserting Fairfax for a more powerful patron.

The King being sold by the Scots "the soldiers," says Yonge, "keep possession, and conduct the King to Herod's Hall, Holmby House; where Peters, like a high priest of the Jews, must confer with him to find what evil he had in him; and though he found him fraught with honour and conscience, yet his Ishmaelitish tongue must be-dirt him, for that HE HAD NOT THE ART OF SPEAKING THE TRUTH —being so long conversant in that of lying and traducing, and therefore reports the King neither for worth nor education worthy of a Justice of the Peace, though Heaven and earth could give him the lie for his pains."

On this curious passage we may remark that it is very likely the earliest accusation of untruthfulness, so often repeated against the unfortunate Charles (especially since the decease of Sir Walter Scott), and may probably have been an original invention of Hugh Peters, who had but poor qualifications for pronouncing judgment in such matters. And from Peters' irreverent, mischievous, and mendacious words, would come the adoption by Cromwell, after he had failed at Hampton Court to bend the King entirely to his will, of the theory that Charles was "so false a man" that he could not be relied on. Of course, those writers who desire to blacken the character of the King need not go back to Hugh Peters to justify their opinion. The dictum of Macaulay, in his introductory chapter of his history, where he announces that he himself prefers Cromwell to Charles, is enough for those who have anti-Royalist prejudices. We consider Hume's estimate of the character of Charles I. (in which he denies the charge of untruthfulness and insincerity) has never yet been disproved by anti-Royalists, whose name is legion. This is not the place to discuss this serious question; and probably few at the present day care even to think about it. Nor will they take the trouble to compare the actual perjuries of the so-called "Statesman" Cromwell with those evasions which the unfortunate King, from the difficult or desperate circumstance he was placed in so often, was occasionally compelled to make. And what sort of faith did his enemies keep with him ?*

* Hume's very important observation that the friends of Charles I., with Clarendon at the head, *never thought it necessary to defend him from the charge of insincerity*, is really decisive. Even the most respectable rebels at the commencement of the Civil War were continually taking advantage of their Sovereign in an underhand way. The enlisting of soldiers in the name of the King to fight against the King is one indisputable instance. King Charles was obliged to *play a game* in self-defence.

CHAPTER XV.

PETERS AND THE KING'S MURDER.

THE details of Peters' career may, perhaps, be elucidated by further discoveries of MSS. in New England. Finding his biographer Yonge's brief account apparently not very wide of the truth, though heated by strong Royalist bias, we shall continue to quote him with regard to the projected murder of the King.

"The Parliament," says Yonge, meaning the Presbyterian part of it, "finding that Oliver[*] and Peters, the grand and prime suggestors of the impious conspiracy, meant to destroy the King, intended to arrest them; but the knavish part of the House" (meaning the Independent

[*] Sir John Berkeley, in his "Memoirs" (q. v.), describes the sudden hostility of Cromwell towards the King, and explains that he went over openly to the party most hostile (viz., to the extreme fanatics); and also specially mentions that Cromwell had the assistance of Peters. The Corkbush field incident took place on November 15th, 1647. After that date Cromwell seems never to have relaxed his hostility to his destined victim, whose actual destruction by violence was planned, according to Berkeley, on the authority of Scout-master Watson, before Christmas, 1647.

or army faction) "giving notice thereof, like a gemini of traitors they prepare themselves for an escape to Cambridge; but the weather proving wet, after hard riding they halted at Ware,* in Middlesex, and entered into a council how to settle the nation in peace, and, in fine, concluded that there was no way left for them but to take the King and bring him to justice for his life . . . to this the whining Saint, Harrison, and the rest say 'Amen.'"

This determination was probably adopted as soon as the mutinous army had been brought into partial subjection at Corkbush field (indeed, Berkeley explains that it was). Oliver, Ireton, and Peters, Yonge continues to record, "held several private meetings at Starkey's house at Windsor—sitting up guarded till two or three in the morning"—plotting treason. These are facts, according to the evidence given at the trial of the regicides, in 1660. Ireton and his wife, the strong-minded Bridget, as we have already mentioned, lodged for some time at Starkie's house, which was close to the Castle, and contained a large room used by Cromwell

---

* Where the mutinous regiments were assembled. As Yonge asserts that Peters repeatedly explained his treasonable actions to his entertainer at Milford, the above statement may contain more truth than Cromwellian admirers might admit.

and the principal officers as a council-room. Peters is reported by Starkie, Junr., at the trial of Peters to be very hostile to the King. Others gave similar testimony. Secret meetings were also held at a Mr. Hildersley's house, ("The Star") in Coleman Street, in the parish of St. Stephen's. Coleman Street was the resort of the dangerous and tyrannical Saints—not only at this time, but after the Restoration.

Isaac Pennington, (illegally) Lord Mayor,* and later on regicide, was a leading spirit there from the time that he headed a mob with a bogus petition with five thousand signatures against Prayer Book and Episcopacy, etc., during the proceedings against Strafford. (See the various accounts of his doings and other strange occurrences in Mr. Freshfield's very remarkable "Parish History, St. Stephen's, Coleman Street.") Mr. Freshfield records that this parish was "the centre of the Cromwellian faction."

At "The Star," in Coleman Street, according to an evidence at the trial of Peters (Wybert Gunter), that house, Mr. Hildersley's, "was a house where Oliver Cromwell and several of that party did use to meet in con-

* After the Battle of Edgehill, 1642.

sultation. . . . They had several meetings. I do remember," continues Gunter, "very well one among the rest, in particular that Master Peters was there. He came in the afternoon, about four o'clock, and was there till ten or eleven at night. I being but a drawer could not hear much of the discourse, but the subject was tending towards the King, when he was a prisoner, for they called him by the name of 'Charles Stuart.' I heard not much of the discourse they were writing, but I guessed it to be something drawn up against the King. I perceived that Mr. Peters was privy to it, and pleasant in the company. . . . Peters wore a great sword." Peters replied: "I never wore a great sword in my life." He also said he had only been at "The Star" once with Nathaniel Fieunes.*

All this evidence goes to corroborate Clarendon's account; and also Berkeley's description of his clandestine meeting with Scout-master Watson at Windsor, who revealed plans like those actually carried out a year later—namely, "Pride's Purge" and the King's destruction.

* Second son of Lord Say, a "root and branch" leader with the younger Vane and others in 1641, *et seq.*—a most active and determined Roundhead. He is said to have been the real author of "Anglia Rediviva," by Clement Walker, who was very likely to know that Joshua Sprigg did *not* write it.

It is very true that the various meetings at Putney plainly indicated bloody intentions towards the King as early as October, 1647—witness the speeches of Goffe* and Rainsborough.

But once the King unhappily got inside Carisbrook, it is plain that Cromwell threw off all remaining disguise, and became the King's declared enemy. There can be little doubt that Adjutant-General Allen (whom Carlyle quotes from "Somer's Tracts") either forgot the exact date of the grand regicidal prayer meeting at Windsor Castle, or *was purposely vague from being under obligations to conceal it.*

Carlyle himself seems dubious about Allen's date; for thus he writes ("Cromwell's Letters,' I., 407):

"At Windsor, *one of those days unknown now which,* etc."

---

* Goffe had, no doubt, what Cromwell would call "the root of the matter" in him. Here are some of his words ("Clarke Papers," I., 283). . . . "It is a scruple amongst the Saints how far they should use the sword; yet God hath made use of them in that work. Many of them have been employed these five or six years. Yet, whatsoever God shall employ us in I could wish this were laid to heart by us, that as we would be called the chosen and faithful that will follow Christ wheresoever He goes, let us tremble at the thought that we should be standing in a direct opposite against Jesus Christ in the work that He is about. . . . Let us inquire whether some of the actions we have done of late . . . do not cross the work of God . . . I mean in our complying with that party which God hath engaged us to destroy" (!) Rainsborough's speeches are to the same effect.

On reference to "Rushworth," under the dates 21st, 22nd, and 23rd December, 1647, we find a description* so like Allen's three days' army consultations, that we conceive it can be nothing else.

The meeting on December 22nd described there lasts from morning till night. It is a meeting of army leaders, and the scene is Windsor Castle. Differences between the officers (indicated in the "Putney Consultations") are made up, and Lieut.-General Cromwell and Mr. PETERS and others "pray fervently and pathetically." Note than an ALLEN† is there (see extract, "Rushworth" *post;* and that Rainsborough, the undisguised deadly enemy of the King, is pardoned, and presently after goes to his command of the Channel Fleet, and almost immediately to Cowes, with the *Constant Reformation.* Perhaps Rushworth, who was probably at this meeting, could have said more about it, had he not been bound by oaths of secrecy. But, indeed, both he and Whitelock occasionally maintain a prudent reserve when ugly facts might have been revealed.

* See next chapter.
† There was, however, another Allen (Francis), who made a good business in the Treasury by clipping the gold coinage; the injured coins were called "Allens." But the Allen mentioned here was probably W. Allen.

Allen,* whom Carlyle quotes with considerable relish, begins his long narrative with allusions to the events of 1647 :

"In the year 1647, you may remember," says he, "we in the army were engaged in actions of a very high nature." Further on he talks about "the King and his party, seeing us not to answer their ends, began to provide themselves by a treaty with the then Parliament set on foot about the beginning of 1648."†

He then describes at length how the army officers "were fit for little but to tear and rend one another" (plainly referring to the state of things at Putney chronicled in the "Clarke Papers"), and how at length three days were devoted to excited discussion. "Accordingly," says he, "we did agree to meet at Windsor Castle *about* the beginning of '48,"‡ and after long description of what took place on that occasion namely, " of prayers, and preaching, and

* Adjutant-General Allen wrote his account in 1659, in Ireland, to stir up Fleetwood. Though Carlyle appears to have a high opinion of Allen, his opinion seems not to have been generally endorsed. Certainly not by Henry Cromwell.

† There was no treaty till the Treaty of Newport, in September, 1648. Perhaps Allen is talking vaguely of the Scots and their projected invasion, and the Presbyterian treaty talked of at Hampton Court in 1647, which gave Cromwell an excuse for his sudden hostility.

‡ New style, *i.e.*, near Christmas, 1647, may be vaguely meant by Allen.

weeping, and repenting" (of ungodly conferences with Royalists), the cold-blooded fanatic goes on to describe how they came to the resolve "*to call Charles Stuart, that man of blood, to account for that blood that he had shed, and the mischief he had done to his utmost against the Lord's Cause and People in these poor nations.*"

This resolve, which they did not dare to publish, and probably swore to conceal—they agreed (with the help of the Lord, of course) to carry out as soon as it could be safely done. Note well what follows, showing previous calculation. The four "dethroning Bills"—as they were most justly called — which had been already discussed at Westminster, were sent down on December 24th, 1647, by the Parliament to the poor King for acceptation. Observe the brutal proceedings when he refuses to sign them on December 28th. He is instantly made a close prisoner (having at that moment designed to escape from his murderous enemies). About January 3rd the Commons debate the dethroning vote of "*No more addresses*," and this is followed by a declaration to set him aside and settle the kingdom without him. At the same time they defamed and slandered him in an amazing manner, publicly accusing him, amongst other crimes, of having betrayed Rochelle, originated the Irish massacre of 1641, and of having poisoned his father, King James (!)*

That Cromwell was the magician at the bottom of all this mischief, his strong speeches, advocating in Parliament these violent proceedings, prove. He had now (if not before) made up his mind to destroy the King. In their blasphemous phraseology these murderous Christians had "sought the Lord in prayer," and had found Him. It was only a question of finding the opportune moment for bringing the Grand Delinquent, who was kept fast under lock and key, to "Justice." A year later that opportunity was found.

How little scruple Oliver ever had in speculating on the removal of the King to another world, we may gather from his reported speech in the early days of the Great Rebellion, that "he would as soon discharge his pistol on the King as on any other man."†

* These were old slanders revived. To those who would really understand this matter of the "four Bills," reference to Clarendon is advised, although Hume's account should also be read, for Hume states correctly the actual items in the "Bills."

† "Clarendon's History"; but quoted in nearly all histories, old or new.

CHAPTER XVI.

Rushworth v. Allen.

We think it advisable to give in a more complete form the report by Rushworth of the three days' meeting of the army leaders and party at Windsor Castle in December, 1647, with further comments upon Allen's "Narrative." Rushworth's account is as follows:

"The General Council of the Army met in the Castle at Windsor: the greatest part of that day (December 21st) was spent in serious declarations by divers officers concerning the present juncture of affairs; many exhortations to unity and affinity, and motion made for passing by offences that had through weakness come from brethren. Major White laid hold of this opportunity, made an acknowledgment that he had spoken some words rashly at Putney, for which he was censured by that Council: desired that he might be looked upon as one that desired the good of the army ; and that being restored to favour he should readily submit to the discipline of the army. This was unanimously approved of, and the Major accordingly readmitted into the General Council.

"Wednesday, December 22nd, was, according to appointment, kept as a solemn fast by the General and officers ; the duties of the day were performed by divers of the officers, amongst whom there was a sweet harmony. The Lieutenant-General, Commissary-General Ireton, Colonel Tichbourn, Colonel Hewson, Mr. Peters, and other officers prayed very fervently and pathetically : this continued from nine in the morning till seven at night. In the evening a motion was made that, whereas Colonel Rainsborough had acted some things which gave offence ; that in regard of his present acknowledgment his former service might not be forgotten, but that the Council would move the General to write to the House that he might be made Vice-Admiral ;* which was assented to by all, and a letter written to Mr. Speaker accordingly.

* Clarendon, after relating the death of Colonel-Admiral Rainsborough, speaks of him thus : "There was not an officer in the army whom Cromwell would not as willingly have lost as this man, who was bold and barbarous to his wish, and fit to be trusted in the most desperate interest " (" Clarendon's History ").

"Thursday, December 23rd, the General Council of the Army again met. . . . This day, also, the Council of War sat about the trial of Captain-Lieutenant Brown, Mr. Crossman, *Mr. Allen*" (N.B.), "and others; but upon acknowledgment of their rash and irregular proceedings, and promise to submit to the discipline of the army for the time to come, they were dismissed and sent to their regiments."*

That Rushworth and W. Allen's narrative (see Carlyle, "Cromwell's Letters," I.) are dealing with the same event and incidents, we think there can be little doubt. The "Clarke Papers," reporting the Putney army meetings, evidently reveal what is brewing. When Cromwell suppressed the open mutinies of the soldiers at Corkbush field, in November, 1647, he no doubt determined his future policy. He no longer had any need of the King's assistance;

How characteristic are the following remarks, ascribed to this rough and ready Saint in the "Clarke Papers": "It may be thought," says Rainsborough, "I am against the King? I am against him or any that would destroy God's people, and I will never be destroyed while I can help myself."

* "Clarke Papers," I., lvii., quoting *Rushworth*, who quotes the "Perfect Diurnal"—which, perhaps, Rushworth had had something to do with. He was probably an active member o "the Press"—then a new institution, which had its birth in 1642.

for the Parliament, at least the major part, was again with him. He became at once, as we say, the open, relentless enemy of his Sovereign, and of all Royalists. The Putney consultations reveal him as endeavouring to restore the discipline of the army—which he himself had destroyed—or, at all events, to secure the obedience of the leading officers. Their fortunes (and their necks) were concerned in the result.

Mr. Carlyle found it convenient to make much of the "Narrative" of Adjutant-General W. Allen, and to accept the date, "about the beginning of 1648," to mean 1648 (o.s.)*

But that acceptation — which contradicts Clarendon and Berkeley (as well as Hume and others)—obliges this question to be considered :

Q. "When did Cromwell become *openly* hostile to the King?" The plain answer must be "About Christmas, 1647." His and Ireton's lead in the House of Commons of the "No more addresses" policy plainly fixes that date —showing both Parliament and army agreed in absolute hostility to the King.

Is it likely that the weeping, and "praying pathetically," and forgiving and embracing,

* *The new style* was used by some *before* the period treated of.

ending in plans for regicide, described by Allen, were deferred until the beginning of 1648 (O.S.), *i.e.*, to about April, 1648, four months later? Or was the King again taken into favour by the Independents during his close confinement at Carisbrook, and after the violently hostile vote of "No more addresses," to be again discarded and doomed in April, 1648? Suppositions too absurd to dream of; when we know that the Independents, after Christmas, 1647, remained steadfastly hostile. Hume's reasoning* about the vote of "No more addresses" cannot, we feel sure, be set aside; and Mr. T. Carlyle was, no doubt, only too glad to contradict Hume and Clarendon by accepting Allen's revelations and doubtful dates. For he was thus enabled to make out a sort of vague defence for the bloodthirsty crew who, as Theodorus Verax aptly said, had for their regicidal plans and deeds no other excuse than the "*base motive of self-preservation.*"†

Of course, with the chance of a new war,

---

* Let the reader refer to any old edition of Hume's "History of England."

† With all due deference, we think Mr. Gardiner makes but an ineffectual attempt, in following Carlyle and accepting Allen's dates, to negative Hume and Clarendon. He seems to find nothing better than a very brief record of a fast held at Windsor, recorded by Whitelock without commentary.

there would also be the chance of considerable plunder and of the perpetuity of the power of the sword, in the probable event of the army prevailing.

The peroration of Allen's "Narrative" (see "Somers' Tracts" or Carlyle's "Cromwell's Letters"), which takes a retrospect of the year ending with the King's murder, is, in our view, one of the most detestable pieces of wicked cant ever penned: "And how the Lord led and prospered us," says this pretended Saint, approved of by Carlyle and followers, "in all our undertakings that year, in this way cutting His work short in righteousness" (!), "making it a year of mercy equal to any since the war began, and making it worthy of remembrance by every gracious soul who was wise to observe the Lord and the operation of His hands—I wish may never be forgotten."

The real conclusion to come to is that there was nothing the least surprising, still less miraculous, in the victory of these sanguinary Pharisees over that helpless prisoner of war, their Sovereign. The poor Royalists of 1648 were ill prepared for the gallant attempt to save King Charles, and to rid themselves of tyrants.

Let us now extinguish the fanatical W. Allen, by quoting Clarendon's opinion of the transactions of the same period. He has just described those murders of loyal noblemen in Palace Yard which followed the King's execution and culminated with that of the "undaunted Capell."

"So ended," says he, "the year one thousand six hundred and forty-eight, a year of the highest dissimulation and hypocrisy, of the deepest villainy, and most bloody treason that any nation was ever cursed with or under: a year in which the memory of all the transactions ought to be rased out of all records; *lest by the success of it atheism, infidelity, and rebellion should be propagated in the world.*"* (Note here that Clarendon dimly perceived what Sir Henry Maine concluded about "Precursors of Revolution," commented on in an early chapter of this book.) Let us, then, to borrow a little of Carlyle's phraseology, endeavour to take leave of "cant"; and permit the blood-stained Independents to stand before us with their gilding rubbed off; and the halo round their sacred heads to disappear and melt into something which the rough and violent, but

* *Italics* not in the original.

crafty and dissembling,* "Lord of the Fens" may have occasionally seen in the lowlands of East Anglia, when he was actively stirring up the Grand Rebellion, namely—the faint but baleful light of an *ignis fatuus!*

* Lucy, the wife of the amiable regicide, Colonel Hutchinson, mentions that Cromwell was *naturally* a dissembler. His great facility in shedding tears, when necessary, perhaps suggests that he may have suffered from hysteria.

CHAPTER XVII.

PETERS' SUPREME ACTS OF TREASON.

WE have mentioned the King's imprisonment at Carisbrook. It may as well be remembered how he got there. And here the determined malevolence and sanguinary projects commence.

In fear of assassination at Hampton Court, inspired by the threatening demeanour of the soldiers, and by Cromwell's actual communications,[*] he departed one stormy night in November, 1647, with Legge, Ashburnham, and Berkeley, and passing through the New Forest at length took refuge for a short time at Titchfield, Hants, with the Dowager Countess of Southampton. By the blundering proceedings

---

[*] King Charles stated in writing that a letter to him, signed E. R., warning him that eight or nine agitators had considered his immediate assassination necessary, did not decide his flight. In this letter, E. R. says these agitators "resolved, for the good of the kingdom, to take your life away; and that to that action they were well assured that Mr. Dell and Mr. PETERS, two of their preachers, *would willingly bear them company;* for they had often said to these agitators your Majesty is but a dead dog," etc. (This letter is quoted in the "Parliamentary History," II., 788.)

of Ashburnham and Berkeley, who were probably both apprehensive for their own safety, he was handed over to Hammond. After the close imprisonment on December 28th, 1647, previously alluded to, he remained guarded for many months, suffering extreme discomfort and many insults. Moreover, he entertained very reasonable apprehensions of assassination. No doubt information (besides what Berkeley communicated) was given him of the sanguinary hatred of the Independents. In what particular manner his murder might be attempted he could not guess. He could not (nor could any reasonable person) contemplate the astounding absurdity and outrageous treason of a mock trial. At the beginning of the troubles, as early as 1641, he had been threatened with the fate of Ahab and Agag; and there had also been repeated publication of narratives of the deaths of Edward II. and Richard II., etc. (These may be seen after some research in the British Museum Library. They are well, printed, and well illustrated with portraits of the doomed Sovereigns looking forth through prison bars.)

There were, indeed, strong accusations of the meditated poisoning of King Charles at

Carisbrook, which led to the trial of Rolph, a violent Independent, who, however, instead of being punished, was promoted.

Yonge makes out that Peters was at Carisbrook Castle on one occasion, and was most offensive to the King; but he appears to have confounded Peters with Hammond, the Governor. The unfortunate Charles had, without the assistance of Peters, a miserable time enough; and in order to regain freedom—or rather to save his life—made several attempts to escape, which, as we all know, failed. He inspired many of his guards and attendants with enthusiastic respect and pity; and some imperilled their lives in order to help him. Hume, an historian not much studied since democratic politics have created new defenders of the "root and branch" Reformers', has a pathetic passage with regard to the Royal prisoner:

"The great source whence the King derived consolation amidst all his calamities was, undoubtedly, religion; a principle which in him seems to have contained nothing fierce or gloomy, nothing which enraged him against his enemies, or terrified him with the dismal prospect of futurity. While everything around

PETERS' SUPREME ACTS OF TREASON   137

him bore a hostile aspect, while friends, family, relations whom he passionately loved, were placed at a distance, and unable to serve him; he reposed himself with confidence in the arms of that Being who penetrates and sustains all nature, and whose severities, if received with piety and resignation, he regarded as the surest pledges of inexhaustible favour."

The proceedings of the King's enemies shortly after the flight from Hampton Court, as soon as they became known, roused the indignation of the mass of his subjects, who, from the time that the Independents became supreme, had begun to repent their rebellious courses. Even before the close imprisonment, December 28th, 1647, they broke out not only in many counties, but also in London, notwithstanding the proximity of the army, the cry being frequently, "For God and King Charles!" and "Down with the Parliament and Army!" accompanied on various occasions by formidable disturbances.

But in April, 1648, things became worse for "the Saints," who were bitterly taunted and ridiculed in pamphlets and diurnals. First, there were petitions for a personal treaty, to set the King again "on the throne of his ancestors." Then, as we all know, came "the second war," which the King and his best friends, Hyde, Orsmond, Capell, etc., had at length determined upon when it should become practicable, in order to compel that settlement which the state of things absolutely required. This was a popular project : for the masses of the people, as well as Royalist gentlemen, open or concealed, detested the tyrannical "Committees"; and the universal military oppression, supported by burdens and taxes before unheard of, drove them nearly out of their senses.

The modern historian views this crisis through nineteenth century spectacles, as if it had been a modern Tory-Radical dispute; but hear Lord Clarendon :

"If a universal discontent and murmuring," says he, "and almost as general a detestation of both Parliament and army, and a most passionate desire that all their follies and madness might be forgotten in restoring the King to all they had taken from him, and in settling that blessed government they had deprived themselves of, could have contributed to His Majesty's recovery, never people were better disposed to erect and repair the building they had so maliciously thrown and pulled down."*

It is pretty certain that a Plebiscite at this time would have set up the King and his party by a large majority.

We have elsewhere attempted to describe, in a work which is (like "The Legend of Montrose") half romance and half history, many of the leading events of the years 1647-8; and cannot, of course, detail here "the 'Prentice Rising," April 10th, 1648; "the Surrey (unarmed) Petition," and the cruel slaughter in Westminster Hall; the rising in Kent; the revolt of the fleet, when that violent Independent, Rainsborough, was dismissed from his command by a "boatswain's mate" (!) But, alas! the risings in Wales, Kent, and Essex, etc. [as well as the gallant defence of Colchester against Fairfax, assisted — or rather governed by Ireton—as also the Scotch invasion, and the attempt of the Northern loyalists] were all found unavailing—proving how little volunteers can do, no matter what their courage and spirit, against regular troops. Parliamentarian vengeance overtook the gallant Royalists in various forms, without a shadow of legality.

* "Clarendon's History," Book XI., beginning of 1648.

Peters' duties as army chaplain seriously recommenced. He prepared Horton's soldiers for the first onslaught against the Welsh Royalists at St. Fagan's, committing there, if we may trust Yonge, an act of cruel deceit towards a young man named Bartlett, his former acquaintance in Holland. He was presently very busy at Pembroke, with Cromwell, where he seems to have acted as a sort of adjutant to the siege train. Afterwards, according to some accounts, he flourished a sword at the Battle of Preston.*

Knowing the feeling of the people, the conquering Roundheads were later on obliged to have a treaty with the King at Newport, Isle of Wight, where they were most particular in making him give his word that he would not attempt to escape while the treaty was going on. For Cromwell, Ireton, and other vindictive Saints resumed their regicidal prayer meetings, and were waiting like crouching tigers—or shall we say like boa-constrictors —ready to crush to death the victim incapable of defence or resistance. There was

---

* Peters appears on another occasion, viz., the invasion of Ireland in 1649, to have been employed by Cromwell in a purely military capacity, namely, in assisting in the despatch of soldiers from Milford Haven.

not a vestige of heroism in their proceedings. Although *force majeur*—namely, the well-paid and recently triumphing soldiery—was on their side, they had not the least scruple in using the poor King's sense of honour, in the matter of his *parole*, to assist their wicked purpose.*

The treaty in the Isle of Wight being ended, and the King having yielded far more than he ever intended—for the Presbyterians cruelly and violently forced his will, hoping by Royal concessions to excuse themselves and vanquish the Independents — the treaty, we say, being ended, the Presbyterian Royalists and the small section of real sympathisers and well-wishers left in the House, voted, after long sittings and excited discussion, that the King's concessions were sufficient to form a basis for the settlement of the kingdom by a large majority.

Then came the act of violence called "*Pride's Purge.*" Colonel Pride (drayman formerly), no doubt by Cromwell's management, though he was not in London at the moment, seized all the so-called Royalists, as they were entering the House to arrange that the King should be

---

* A curious commentary on the theory of the doubtful value of the poor King's word.

brought to London, in proper state, to "treat with his Parliament."

Every one knows how the King, early one morning in November, was violently seized at Carisbrook—a basely dishonourable* proceeding, in spite of all the strange attempts to condone it—and was conducted by armed force to Windsor, and finally to London in January, 1648 (o.s.), to be tried for his life (if the pretended legal farce can be really called a trial).

At the trial of Peters and the regicides in October, 1660, came out the fact, sorrowfully alluded to by Edmund Burke, in his famous essay on the French Revolution, of "Peters triumphing." "I'll warrant you we'll whisk him!" are the words put into his mouth by Dr. Yonge. Another authority reports Peters riding triumphantly, somewhere near Brentford, before a coach in which the poor King sat alone.

The savagery of the soldier guards is strongly painted by the assertion that, for taking off his hat to the King, who returned the salute, a passing loyal subject, who was

---

* As the King told them to their faces, at the mock trial in Westminster Hall.

mounted, was ridden at by the troopers and overthrown, horse and all, at the side of the road.

Peters was very busy before the King's trial. After " Pride's Purge," Clement Walker describes how, "about three of the clock in the afternoon, Hugh Peters, with a sword by his side (but not the sword of St. Peter), came into the Queen's Court to take a list of the prisoners' names, by order from the General (*i.e.*, Fairfax), as he said. When being demanded 'by what authority they were imprisoned?' he answered, 'By the power of the sword.' Night being come, the imprisoned members (forty-one in number) were conveyed away to a dwelling called Hell."*

Evelyn has some severe remarks against Peters preaching against the King in the "painted chamber" previous to the trial.

Peters at the trial, according to more than one account, encouraged Axtell—a violent Cromwellian colonel—who afterwards committed formidable atrocities in Ireland, and a massacre upon a grand scale—forced the soldiers to cry "Justice!" and "Execution!" and

* "Under the Exchequer," *Clarendon*. This locality is alluded to in Butler's "Hudibras." It was a kind of *restaurant*.

beat them when they refused. Amongst other pieces of presumption, Yonge relates "with what triumphing insolence he did settle the chair* of Fate for the King to sit in at his trial before the Court of High Injustice!"

"High Injustice" is a good phrase. Algernon Sidney (a Republican) truly said that "not only no King could be tried by that tribunal, but no man," which was, indeed, a paraphrase of the King's actual words to his pretended Judges. Sir P. Warwick remarks that at the time of the trial "Peters was really the King's jailer."

It has been asserted that Peters never forgave the King for refusing to allow him to preach before him (query at Newmarket† or St. Albans). This refusal, perhaps, puzzled the brain of the arrogant Peters, who had been several times invited to preach before the "schismatic Lords and Commons," and had in earlier times been adored in the City, at least by his female auditory. Amongst concessions made by Peters, it is, however, considered creditable that he allowed and procured the

* This identical chair was exhibited at the Stuart Exhibition some few years ago.

† Whitelock mentions that Peters had many interviews with the King at Newmarket.

attendance of Juxon upon the King just before his execution.

Peters—we learn from the "State Trials," as well as from Yonge and others—preached several times against the King, before, during, and after the trial. The places recorded are at St. Margaret's, Westminster;* the "painted chamber," Whitehall, St. James's, and the scene of his earlier ministrations, St. Sepulchre's (sad suggestive name!) At one or all of these places, as has been already mentioned in these pages, he compared the King to Barabbas (whom the people wished to be released), and the soldiers to Christ (!) At St. Margaret's Cromwell was seen to laugh at this impious piece of humour.*

We reserve some brief reflections upon the King's murder to that portion of our remarks which touches upon the inquiry into regicide guilt. We must, in the meantime, proceed to Ireland with the "godly" army which went there in the autumn of 1649, to fight—not the

* Peters appears to have commenced these pulpit denunciations of the King on the 22nd of December, 1648. On this occasion he is said to have concluded his discourse thus: "Kneeling and weeping, and lifting up his hands, be begged (the Commons), in the name of the people of England, to execute justice upon that great Barabbas of Windsor." He probably repeated the sermon several times.

Irish or the Catholics, who were supposed to have anything to do with the massacre of Protestants in 1641—but the loyal forces under Ormond, which viewed the King's trial and execution with indignation.

CHAPTER XVIII.

" Drogheda Quarter."

AFTER the death of King Charles, Peters went as Cromwell's chaplain to Ireland. Owen accompanied him as assistant. Peters "prepared"* the soldiers for the assault of Drogheda. He also wrote the first official report of the massacre. It is printed, and the small sheet is adorned with the State arms. It may be remarked that the phrases " minister of God's Word " and " none spared " seem curiously to jar.

Peters' Report.

Letter from Ireland, read in the House of Commons on Friday, September 29th, 1649.

From Mr. Hugh Peters, minister of God's Word and chaplain to the Lord Lieutenant Cromwell.

---

* " A little before Tredah," says one account, Peters preached on the forty-fifth Psalm : " Thy arrows are very sharp, and the people shall be subdued unto Thee."

"Sir,—The truth is Tredah* is taken; three thousand five hundred fifty and two slain and sixty-four of ours.

"Colonel Castle and Captain Simmons of note.

"Ashton, the Governor, killed; none spared.

"We have also Trim and Dundalk, and are marching on Kilkenny.

"I came now from giving thanks in the great church. We have all our army well landed.

"I am, Sir, yours,

"HUGH PETERS."

Yonge, Peters' biographer, asserts that men, women, and children were murdered in gates and steeples at Drogheda. It is quite certain that men, at all events, were *burnt alive* in St. Peter's Church, who had fled up into the steeple. It is not improbable that some of their wives (and even children) may have joined them there, as a supposed place of security; and Anthony à Wood has a story† of ladies in the vaults of the church.

* Drogheda was always called Tredah at that time. It is the phonetic spelling of the Irish pronunciation of the name.

† Thomas à Wood (Anthony's brother), a Roundhead soldier in Cromwell's army, asserted that the poor men in St. Peter's Church carried children with them up into the steeple as a sort of protection, and that these, as well as the men, were killed (and burnt). The story of the young lady "richly dressed" and

To churches frightened women are very apt to betake themselves when houses become unsafe. Some of the wives of Ormond's officers and soldiers might have been there. Mr. Gardiner thinks it improbable that they would wear jewellery on such an occasion; but where is the improbability? Jewellery is a very portable kind of property, and at least might secure ransom from humane soldiers. It could not be left in houses which soldiers were sacking. While the terrified women may have remained in the crypt, the poor men fled up into the steeple.

Cromwell, in order to get his victims down, asked them to "render to mercy." But they would understand that he meant "Colchester mercy," which was succeeded by shooting two commanders,* decimating the soldiers and selling the rest as slaves to the West Indies and Africa. They were therefore not likely to trust to his offer; at all events, the church was set on fire and they were burnt. It is singular, considering Peters' connection with

wearing, or in the possession of jewellery, who was fiendishly murdered by a soldier to whom she knelt for mercy, seems by no means impossible. What happened to her companions is not stated.

* And murdering a third some time afterwards in cold blood by sentence of the illegal High Court of Justice.

these horrors, that the church was called St. Peter's, being dedicated to that Saint. Mr. Gardiner quotes a pamphlet which reports an oath attributed to one of the poor victims in the throes of mortal anguish. But he might have found the same relation in Cromwell's own letter, which Carlyle printed without comment —or rather with subsequent approval. From this long letter ("Cromwell's Letters," II., 188) we extract this short passage: "Divers officers and soldiers being fled over the bridge into the other part of the town, where about one hundred of them possessed St. Peter's Church steeple . . . these being summoned refused. Whereupon *I ordered the steeple of St. Peter's Church to be fired; when one of them was heard to say, in the middle of the flames, ' God d—n me, God confound me; I burn, I burn.'* "

This is fiendish; the inference plainly being that Cromwell concludes that such profane individuals were rightly served, and need not be much regretted.

Perhaps it is as well to quote one more fragment of the same letter, which tends to hint that as Popery was connected with St. Peter's Church, all those who were destroyed there were in the same category with those who were burnt, *i.e.*, they were righteously destroyed.

"It is remarkable," writes Cromwell, "that these people at the first set up the Mass in some places in the town that had been monasteries; but afterwards grew so insolent that the last Lord's Day before the storm, the Protestants were thrust out of the great church called St. Peter's, and they had public Mass there: *and in this very place near one thousand of them were put to the sword fleeing thither for safety.** I believe all the friars were knocked on the head promiscuously but two, the one of which was Father Peter Taaff, brother to the Lord Taaff whom the soldiers took next day and made an end of. The other was taken in the Round Tower, under the repute of a lieutenant; and when he understood that the officers in that tower had no quarter, he confessed he was a friar: but that did not save him" ("Cromwell's Letters," II., 200).

We may observe here, that though Crom-

* It seems not impossible, as Cromwell does not distinguish sexes, that women were among these one thousand put to the sword; and that Yonge, who may have heard it from Peters, is correct in his statement. There was no scruple about murdering Irish women after Naseby.

well was great at praying, preaching, and slaughtering, his sense of humour was small. "All the friars," he writes, "were knocked on the head promiscuously but two," and these two were "made an end of." One might have supposed that the exceptions might have come better off. They only had the privilege of being slain in cold blood.

Though these acts of Cromwell and his associates at Drogheda have been silvered over by attempted palliations and excuses, it is pretty plain that the only explanation or excuse that can be offered is *that the design was to terrorise;* and that no scruples were entertained about the mode of carrying it out. Nor do we know the full extent of the atrocities committed. There were few left to tell the tale. We can well imagine that under the rule of the severe Republicans of that day it was dangerous in the highest degree to comment in writing upon their lawless acts; and after the Restoration so many Independents and Parliamentarians becoming, or feigning to be repentant, details of crime were not much dwelt upon, after summary justice had been done upon a small number of guilty men. Pepys shows how completely cant (*i.e.*, the ostentatious pretence of superior piety) went out of fashion. The sullen fanatics wisely held their tongues for the most part, while the mass of the population, both high and low, turned all their thoughts to amusement and forgetfulness of the grim, sordid tyranny of "the Saints."

Carte's brief account of "Drogheda Quarter," at the end of which he quotes Ormond's views, is probably as near the truth as any other. We may note that Mr. Gardiner, though he lets off his admired Oliver as easily as he can, has the frankness to give no support to the fiction that the Drogheda slaughter (of English officers and disciplined Irish Royalist soldiers) was executed in revenge of the Irish massacres of 1641.

The following is extracted from Carte's "Life of Ormond," a book which, from its great length, few people care to read,' though it contains a number of strange facts:

Cromwell "began to batter the place on Sunday, the 9th (September); and having continued the battery from that time till Tuesday, about four in the afternoon, a large breach was made near St. Mary's Church, which he judged available. The assault was given, and his men were twice repulsed; but in the third attack

Colonel Wall, being unhappily killed at the head of his regiment, his men were so dismayed thereby as to listen before they had need to the enemy's offering them quarter, admitting them upon those terms, and thereby betraying themselves and their fellow-soldiers to slaughter. All the officers and soldiers of Cromwell's army promised quarter to such as would lay down their arms, and performed it as long as any place held out ; which encouraged others to yield. But when they had once all in their power, and feared no hurt that could be done them, Cromwell being told by Jones " (Governor of Dublin) "that he had now the flower of the Irish army " (*i.e.*, Ormond's army, some of which were English) " in his hands, gave orders that no quarter should be given,* so that his soldiers were forced, many of them against their will, to kill their prisoners. The brave Governor, Sir A. Aston, Sir Edward Verney, the Colonels Warren, Fleming, and Byrne were killed in cold blood ; and, indeed, all officers except some of the least consideration that escaped by miracle. The Marquis of Ormond, in his letter to the King

---

* This would account for Peters' computation of the slain ; only sixty-four of the besiegers, but three thousand five hundred and fifty-two of the besieged slaughtered, no doubt, most of them, after having surrendered their arms.

and Lord Byron, says : 'That on this occasion Cromwell exceeded himself, and anything he had ever heard of, in breach of faith and bloody inhumanity ; and that the cruelties exercised there for five days after the town was taken would make as many several pictures of inhumanity as are to be found in the Book of Martyrs and in the relation of Amboyna.'"

Peters' sermon, a week or two later, in the great church in Dublin (probably St. Patrick's), must have been a peculiar discourse.

The following quotation from a diurnal gives a remarkable colouring to Cromwell's finishing touches to his sanguinary work, when we reflect that the men who were called "traitors," and whose heads were "hanged upon poles," were honourable gentlemen, true to their oaths of allegiance; one of them, indeed, Aston, having been Governor of Reading and afterwards of Oxford for the murdered Charles.

Extract from a letter from Dublin, September 14th, 1649.

"There are sixteen of the chief of their heads cut off, and sent to Dublin to be hanged upon poles as traitors; and it is said that among the rest is Aston, the Governor; and the Lord Grandison, young Villiers and Armstrong (that apostate), and young Varney and Goodwin, and others.

"A list of the officers and soldiers slain during the storming of Drogheda: Sir Arthur Aston, Governor; Sir Edward Varney, Lieutenant-Colonel to Ormond's regiment; Colonel Fleming, of horse; Lieut.-Colonel Finglass, of horse; Major Fitzgerald, of horse; eight captains, lieutenants, and cornets of horse; Colonels Wain, Walls, and Byron, of foot, with other lieutenants, majors, etc. The Lord Taafe's brother, an Augustine fryar; forty-four captains and all their lieutenants and ensigns, two hundred and twenty troopers, two thousand five hundred foot soldiers, besides staff officers and chirurgeons, and *many inhabitants*."

Such are the outlines of the dark story of "Drogheda Quarter."

Cromwell, as everybody knows, had the assurance to ask the so-called "Lord President" Bradshaw (who some months before sat with an iron-lined hat at the upper end of Westminster Hall, to condemn his King to death), and also to ask William Lenthall, Speaker of the Rump Parliament, "to give God all the glory of this great mercy" (!)

We trust that before the close of the nineteenth century of the Christian era, most of the rational people of these islands will cease to revere the teachings of the "fierce Scotch Puritan," and decline to venerate St. Cromwell, with his Scriptural phraseology and his deeds of fanaticism, craft, treason, and blood. The exploits of Blake abroad cannot redeem the crimes of his master at home.

CHAPTER XIX.

PETERS "IN EXCELSIS."

IT is enough to have lingered over the first Cromwellian victory in Ireland in which Peters played his part. Wexford horrors followed. Yonge relates that men, women, and children were "driven into the sea."

Cromwell gives a glowing account of this success, and chronicles the amount of plunder —houses full of goods, the owners of which had been destroyed. The wretched Peters got his share of the good things. At Clonmel, subsequently, the poor murdered victims at Drogheda were, to a certain extent, avenged. When a breach had at length been made by Cromwell's artillery, there was no possibility of offering delusive promises of quarter. A deadly obstruction confronted the surprised assailants, and two thousand of the "godly" army were shot down by the valiant Northern Irish Royalist defenders, who succeeded in making their escape, leaving only unarmed people in the town. Not long after this, Cromwell, who had been ill, quitted Ireland. Peters preceded him. Ireton was left as deputy. The Cromwellian soldiers, mostly troublesome "levellers," whom the usurping Government were not sorry to be rid of, came to a sad end. Many of them, with their cruel and cold-blooded leader, Henry Ireton, died of the plague.

One of the officers, the murderous Axtell, who, as Lingard mentions, assassinated poor Irish women, besides effecting much unjustifiable slaughter, survived, to become a Cromwellian Saint, dying glorious and unrepentant at Tyburn after the Restoration.

"Rich with the plunder of Wexford," says Yonge, "and affrighted with guilt, Peters procures a command from Oliver, and goes as a colonel to Wales, to raise a regiment." Then comes an illness, which led to his acquaintance with his kind biographer, to whom he was introduced by a soldier, whose name has not much sound of temperance, for Yonge calls him Captain *Brandy* (it was probably Brandly*). "Peters," says Yonge, "remaining

* Who shared in the Drogheda massacres.

in my house ten weeks with horses and servants, all upon free quarter" (free quarter however much the public complained of it, was the usual privilege of the "godly" army). Peters, according to New England authorities, was at this time Governor of Milford Haven.

The motto on his colours, according to Yonge, was: "*No King, no Lords, we are engaged*"—a motto which shows his intimate acquaintance with the plans of Oliver and those of the Council of State.

Yonge asserts that he had continual confidential conversations with Peters at Milford, who laid bare his many treasons.

Oliver Cromwell's wife seems not to have had much confidence in Peters. Yonge, at least, informs us that she drew up articles against him. Peters, however, got clear of her toils, sheltered, it is presumed, by the ægis of Oliver.

By the way, we discover a curious tenacity on the part of Mrs. Cromwell in retaining what she had got, and which shows her to have apparently imbibed some portion of Oliver's courage (or to have had strong faith in the pious opinion that "the Saints should possess the earth").

At the Restoration, when she appeared to have been found occupying Worcester House (which was on the riverside, near the present site of Beaufort Buildings), she refused to deliver up the title-deeds of Raglan, *i.e.*, the Marquis of Worcester's estate—which she and Oliver had long battened upon—until peremptorily ordered by the Parliament.

In 1651 Peters was appointed a member of a "Committee on Law," *i.e.*, for its reform. Whitelock, who elsewhere occasionally speaks well of Cromwell's favourite, probably because he *was* Cromwell's favourite, bears witness (as Lockhart did later on) to Peters' presumption and ignorance. "I was often," he remarks, "advised with by some of the members of this committee, and none of them was more active in this business than Peters, the minister, who understood little of the law, but was very opinionative, and would frequently mention some proceedings of law in Holland, wherein he was entirely mistaken."*

Mr. Felt records that Peters "advised when a proper code was finished, to burn all the old records, yea, even those in the Tower, the monuments of tyranny." Peters here para-

* "Whitelock's Memorials," p. 521.

phrases the words put by the author of "The Shakespeare Plays" into the mouth of Jack Cade:

"Away! burn all the records of the realm—my mouth shall be the Parliament of England!"* But in case of laws framed by an English rebel to supplant Acts of Parliament and other State documents, a destructive policy was not so absurd as it seems. Perhaps all the regicides were glad to see Peters on 'such a committee—if it were only to put forward the idea of erasing such Acts of Parliament as the 25th Edward III.

Happily, there were men like Whitelock, not so far involved in treason, who had lawyer's prejudices, and did not believe that the "Commonwealth" would last for ever; so "the Records" were spared.

It is not to be understood that the eminent Selden was a convinced Roundhead, any more than many other men of a certain age, or of cautious temperament. Clarendon has mentioned that not a few good men remained in London to help the King's party secretly, who, had they been younger, might have gone to

* Was the idea inspired by reminiscences of "The Globe" and "Blackfriars"?

York, or later to Oxford. It is probable also that the fear inspired by the execution of Strafford, and the fury of the "root and branch" reform party, was the cause of the defection of more than one noble lord, who in his heart would have preferred passive obedience to his Sovereign and conformity to the Church. Two years' experience of the consequences of rebellion were sufficient to disgust Essex and Manchester, who probably at the end of 1644 wished that they had never drawn the sword in behalf of "the Good Old Cause."

CHAPTER XX.

HUGH PETERS AT DUNKIRK.

ONE of the closing incidents in Peters' days of prosperity is his visit to Dunkirk, where he was chaplain, political agent, self-appointed ambassador, and what not. "He hath laid himself forth," says Colonel Lockhart, "in great charity and goodness in sermons, prayers, and exhortations, in visiting and relieving the sick and wounded. And in all these profitably applying the singular talent God hath bestowed upon him, to *the chief ends proper for our auditory.** For he hath not only showed the soldiers their duty to God, and pressed it home to them, I hope, to good advantage ; *but hath likewise acquainted them with their obligations of obedience to His Highness' Government, and affection to his person.* . . . It were superfluous to tell your Lordship the story of our present condition, either as to civil govern-

---
* The passages italicised are not so in Lockhart's letter.

ment, works, or soldiery. He" (meaning Peters) "who hath studied all these more than any I know here, can certainly give the best account of them. Wherefore, I commit the whole to his information, and beg your Lordship's casting a favourable eye upon such propositions he will offer to your Lordship for the good of this garrison. I am—may it please your Lordship — your most humble, faithful, and obedient servant,
"WILL LOCKHART."

In a postscript, written in his own hand, Lockhart informs "my Lord" (*i.e.*, Secretary Thurloe) that Peters delayed going persistently, and interviewed Cardinal Mazarin frequently.

"I," says Lockhart, "had a *care that he did not importune him with too long speeches.* He returns loaden with an account of all things here, and hath undertaken *every man's business* . . . *if it were possible to get him to mind preaching and to forbear troubling himself with other things*, he would certainly prove a very fit minister for soldiers . . . he hath often insinuated to me his desire to stay here if he had but a call. Some of the officers have been with me to that purpose, but I have shifted him so handsomely as I hope he will not be displeased. For I have told him that the greatest service he can do is to go to England and carry on his propositions, and to serve us in all other interests which he hath undertaken with so much zeal.

"July 8—18th, 1658."

The death of Peters' great patron and quondam bosom friend, Oliver Cromwell, not very long after this, must have disturbed Peters very considerably. He wrote very frequently to Henry Cromwell in Ireland subsequently; but the *Interregnum* and the hitherto triumphant reign of "the Saints" was coming to an end.

CHAPTER XXI.

Peters' Decline and Fall.

We have various mentions of Hugh Peters in New England documents during the Protectorate.

Roger Williams, the formerly persecuted Baptist, saw him at Whitehall in 1654, and states that " Peters preacheth the same doctrine as formerly, but not so zealous as some years since, and cries out against New England rigidities and persecutions . . . their injustice to himself, and their unchristian dealings with him in excommunicating his wife. All this he told me *in his lodgings at Whitehall, which I was told was Canterbury's; but he himself told me that that library* where we came together was Canterbury's, and given him by Parliament."† (This library was given to Peters

---

* "All my books at Lambeth," Laud records, " were, by order of the House of Commons, taken away, and carried I know not where; but are, it is commonly said, for the use of Peters."

† Italicised as being in proof of the theory that *pseudo St. Peter* was the head of the Cromwellian Church.

after Laud's execution.) The "King's Library," many actual volumes of which are now in the British Museum Library, was also given to Peters after the King's murder.*

"Your father," continues Williams to Winthrop, Junr.," meaning Peters, "and all the people of God, are now in the saddle and at the helm. Some cheer their spirits up with the impossibility of another fall or turn . . . so doth Major-General Harrison" (though now, or a little later, by the way, a prisoner for mutiny against Cromwell). "Surely, sir, he is a . . . most deserving, heavenly man ; but most highflown for the kingdom of Saints and the fifth Monarchy."

But Vane, Williams reports, was looking forward to the general persecution of "the Saints," and " the slaughter of the witnesses."

The excommunication of Peters' wife, "Deliverance Peters," is curious, for she had gone mad, as we learn from several accounts. She had been once or twice sent backwards and forwards across the Atlantic. On one occasion Peters writes, "Have an eye to my

* Clement Walker also notices that after the murder of Charles I., "The King's Library at St. James's was given, I hear, to that ignorant stage-player, Hugh Peters" ("Hist. of Independency," Part II., 133).

wife"; on another he exclaims: "Oh that I had remained in New England, or had not this wife sent back to me!" A letter from Peters shows that "the authorities" in New England had sold off all his property there at a low rate; and sent to England a remnant which was of no value.

At the fall of Tumble-down-Dick, as Richard Cromwell was called, fears began to fall upon the "godly" party, who were, of course, well aware that by the well-known laws of England (plainly announced to them by Judge Jenkins in 1648) most of them were guilty of high treason (by the 25th Edward III., for having *levied war against the King*, etc.)

Mr. Davenport, Peters' former associate, writes from Newhaven, September 28th, 1659, that he hears from England that " Mr. Hugh Peters is distracted, and, under some horror of conscience, crying out of himself as damned, and confessing haynous *(sic)* actings."

This report somewhat agrees with Yonge's statement that Peters about this time "announced himself to be Antichrist, and that he must shortly be destroyed."

Peters, however, so far recovered as to be able to combat Restoration ideas from the pulpit. Monk was obliged to sit and hear him preach at St. Alban's, in favour of the continuance of the government of "the Saints." Monk was then, at the end of 1659 (o.s.), on his march to London.

Scott and Robertson, spies and agents of "the Rump," bored holes in the door or wall of the General's "lodgings" at St. Alban's, to discover what he was generally saying or doing.*

After the Restoration a peremptory order was sent to Peters to surrender the library of Archbishop Laud, and also, of course, the King's Library at St. James's.†

At the Restoration Peters naturally tried to hide. An order was sent from the House of Commons for his arrest. Once his name was coupled with that of Vane, once with Hulett, and once with Joyce. The two last were suspected, as Peters was himself, of being—one or other of them—the masked executioner of the King. Some swore to having seen Peters on

* "Life of Monk."

† Peters, in reply to the inquiry made on behalf of Charles II. about the King's Library at St. James's, said that in 1648 he preserved it from the encroachments of the soldiers; that it was in his custody three or four months; that he left it nothing damaged or injured, and delivered the key of it to General Ireton.

the scaffold among those wearing masks. This was the one thing that Peters seemed anxious to prove his innocence* of at the trial. Possibly he thought that circumstance would be the only one which could be made a capital charge. He was arrested by Stephen Harris, constable of St. Thomas' Parish, in Southwark. When found he denied his identity, and called himself "Thomson." It is curious that this was the assumed name that the great Nelson chose to hide his identity, when making a communication which he wished to keep private. The district where Peters concealed himself was one frequented by actors in the days of his connection with "Shakespeare's Company."

We may remark that if Thomason had anything to do with the "King's Library," did not Peters probably attempt to personate him?†

At the trial, which we have already alluded to, Peters set up an *alibi* for January 30th,

---

* This probably explains his reported assertion, at his execution at Charing Cross, that he had *no hand* in the death of the King.

† Though not mentioned in the "National Biography," it has, we think, been stated that King Charles originally ordered Thomason, as early as 1640-1, to collect the political pamphlets. Thomason was evidently a strong Royalist; but in his collection of pamphlets from 1640 to 1660 seems scarcely to have omitted any Roundhead composition.

1648, and proved he was ill at St. James's Palace. This, at least, Yonge seems to think true; but says he feigned himself ill, fearing a tumult. A rescue of the poor King had been planned, but appears to have been prevented by the pretence of a reprieve. Of course, with the huge phalanx of force, a rescue would have been practically impossible, as the designs of the Royalists (then completely cowed and subdued by the disastrous ending of the second war) were easy to thwart. As to the suspicion of Peters having been the executioner of Charles I., it seems improbable that Cromwell (who was the manager-in-chief of the tragedy, though he only sat with Ireton at a window of the Banqueting Hall as a spectator) would be likely to entrust the all-important stroke of vengeance to the arm of a preacher sixty years of age, who was frequently ill.

If Richard Brandon were not the executioner, as Sir Henry Ellis believed, it may have been Joyce, that stalwart agitator, who had been employed by Cromwell (query and Fairfax*) to seize the King at Holdenby. If

* The Lord Capell seemed to think that Fairfax did not quite clear himself when taxed by the King. But Fairfax admits himself that his name was often made use of by subordinates.

PETERS' DECLINE AND FALL

Peters was not on the scaffold, perhaps Hulett, or Cromwell's secretary, Spavin, was the other masked individual.

We may observe here that the trial and murder of Charles I. were as much the result of the rage and fury of the army and the Independents as of policy.

The execution was especially vindictive. "We will cut off his head with the crown on it," was the angry and contemptuous speech of Oliver. And the reason why "the open space in front of Whitehall" was chosen as the scene of that act of wickedness, was because the very numerous petitions to the Lords and Commons in 1648 generally made use of the phrase, "that King Charles be brought to London in freedom, honour, and safety." The general cry of the poor deceived, but now awakened and repentant people, who found too late what miseries rebellion had brought, was, "Bring *home* our King!"*

Mr. Gardiner's candour—though some of his reflections upon the trial and execution of the King to some people must appear either

---

* No wonder "the Saints" were alarmed and angry. Even if their lives were not threatened, the lucrative positions many of them held, and the spoils of the Church and "malignant" party could no longer be enjoyed with safety.

astounding or ludicrous—allows that ropes were fixed to the scaffold to drag the martyr down to the block in case of resistance.

It was worthy of the jesting Peters, of the rude, violent, and unscrupulous Cromwell, and of the cruel, cold-blooded Ireton, to answer the people as they did; namely, to "bring home" the King as a prisoner, and put him to death as a pretended criminal in front of his own house!

Posterity will eventually consider the late Thomas Carlyle's attempt to make light of, or rather to glorify what was really an act of extreme baseness, as little short of disgraceful.*

Before closing our remarks on Hugh Peters, we shall devote a page or two to the peculiar events which have occurred at the scene of his American ministrations.

---

* See "Cromwell's Letters," II., 129, where with other compliments, Mr. T. Carlyle hails the regicides with the words: "Honour to the brave" (!) But who can say? Perhaps the Chelsea sage, all through his "monumental" work, was only laughing in his sleeve, and no more believed in Oliver's claim to saintship than that the "Squire Papers" were genuine.

CHAPTER XXII.

A Record of Salem.

LOCAL accounts of SALEM* reveal some historical curiosities deserving of special notice. Though it has been already mentioned in these pages, we may remind readers that the dominating and persecuting spirit of the founders of the Massachusetts Bay Company was developed under the ministration of Hugh Peters. John Endicott, who headed the first body of adventurers, landed at SALEM on September 6th, 1628. He was the first Governor, and was succeeded by Winthrop.

SALEM, according to local authorities, was considered the capital. Vane the Younger and his government we have already mentioned.

The spirit of *Independency* which had its rise in the Great Rebellion (instructively discoursed upon by Clement Walker in 1648) seems to have haunted SALEM—the scene of

* "Visitor's Guide to Salem," and "Annals of Salem."

pseudo St. Peter's ministrations in a singular manner; as if the ghost of the man who is called by the American historian Bancroft "the fiery Hugh Peters" had taken up its fixed abode there. When we come to examine the details of considerable events in the world's history, it really seems as if the genius of history or some invisible agency occasionally contrived something like pre-ordained jests. The remarkable anagrams on the names of Nelson and Wellington are too well known to allude to here. From SALEM, a presumed City of Peace, a great deal of war has been developed, commencing with Hugh Peters' apostleship to the old country, and his departure on Cromwell's Day (3rd of September).

We learn from Bancroft, as well as from other historians, that the spirit of persecution which had its first headquarters at SALEM in the time of Charles I., did not subside during the Commonwealth and Protectorate, but was further developed in the reign of Charles II.

In the reign of William III. SALEM was the chief scene of the terrible witchcraft delusion. When we come to the War of Independence, it is SALEM which seems to lead the dance. It must not be forgotten, in justification of "obstinate old George III.," that when things came to a crisis the great majority of the best people in Boston sailed thence for Nova Scotia and other places, because they would have nothing to do with what they characterised as a "Wicked Rebellion."

Of course, worthy successors and representatives of the early Saints remained behind.

At SALEM, October 5th, 1774, "assembled the first Provincial Congress, which passed, during its session, a vote renouncing the authority of the British Parliament; the first official act of the Province putting itself in open opposition to the Home Government."

More remarkable, perhaps, is the following item:

"On 26th February, 1775, the citizens of SALEM offered the first armed resistance to the English Government, in assembling at Northbridge, and forbidding the progress of Colonel Leslie and a body of British soldiers."

Another record:

"During the revolutionary war SALEM furnished large numbers of men to fill the ranks of the army, and fitted out at least one hundred and fifty-eight vessels as privateers."

Again: "In the war of 1812, forty armed

vessels of the two hundred and fifty furnished by the whole country were from SALEM."

" The vessels of SALEM," says the same authority from which we quote, " were the first to display the American flag, and open trade with St. Petersburg and other places."

Although Anglican worship was, of course, presumed to be authorised and supported by the (however very peculiar) charter of the Massachusetts Bay Company mysteriously obtained from Charles I., Anglican worship was never permitted until the reign of Charles II. (query if then?)

At SALEM " in 1777, Episcopal service was suspended, owing to the passing by the Legislature of a law forbidding the reading of it under a penalty of one hundred pounds and one year's imprisonment. The church in that town was ransacked and much damaged."

An Episcopal church, however, was erected in 1833 and dedicated to (the real) St. Peter.

It was not enough that the crowning event of the commencement of actual war with England should be chronicled in local history. The following visible testimony probably exists at the present day, as it did thirty or forty years ago :

"Northbridge," says the same local authority before quoted . . . is a small bridge across the north river, at the entrance to (North) SALEM. On the north side of the bridge a tall flagstaff bears the inscription :

"RETREAT OF COLONEL LESLIE. February 26th, 1775. At this point, on Sabbath-day, the townspeople assembled and forbade the further advance of Colonel Leslie."

Had Peters survived up to this period, can we doubt that he would have made a jest or two on these important events? The name of Leslie would have recalled the Presbyterian general who fought at Marston Moor and was defeated at Dunbar ; but there is a decided opening for witticism in the mention of Northbridge and the north side of the river. *Omne bonum ab aquilone*, the quondam fool of Shakespeare's Company would probably have quibbled: "Promotion cometh neither from the east nor from the west, nor yet from the south."

We have read somewhere that SALEM was also to the fore when Federals and Confederates were about to commence that great struggle whose intensity is seen in the very large pension list which has been one of the results.

A little ice may now be applied to the record of so many fiery reminiscences. Hugh Peters once preached a great sermon to the text, "At Eron was much water." This discourse was delivered on a hill near Wenham Lake, which in later years has plentifully supplied old country refrigerators.

What other great men SALEM has developed we have not discovered; but as a good set-off against the glowing unction left behind by Hugh Peters, we may mention that one Immortal at least claimed SALEM as his native place—no other than the truly illustrious historian, Prescott.*

We should not be surprised to learn that, beyond traditions, there is not much at the present time to remind one of past violence and intolerance in the once peculiar little New England town which bears the name of SALEM.

* The eminent Mr. Phelps, the Nestor of the United States, so well known and so much esteemed in this country, was also born at Salem.

CHAPTER XXIII.

Exit Hugh Peters.

ALTHOUGH accounts are conflicting, we think we may be permitted to say that Peters was not brave* when he suffered at Charing Cross. Cooke appears to have tried to encourage him. But Cooke had acknowleged the justice of his sentence. Peters did not. None of the others did. On the contrary, they justified their acts —it is said—in expectation of another rebellion which would avenge their deaths and set the Saints up again. Axtell—a man who, as we mentioned, perpetrated great barbarities—was exceptionally audacious. Vane expected to come again, at the right hand of Christ, to judge the Royalists and the rest of the wicked.

Some said that Peters was drugged or half drunk. One account states that he was drinking a cordial at the place of execution. He preached a sermon in Newgate, amidst great

* Certainly the executioner did all he could to intimidate him.

interruptions, just before his death. His language was most grotesque, and not a little blasphemous. On the ladder, at the place of execution—which was where the equestrian statue of Charles I. now stands—he tried to address the people, but they refused to listen to him. "The people are so satisfied," writes Nicholas, the much valued Secretary of State to King Charles I., that "they even shout with joy on the death of the most hardened traitors."

How different is Mr. Felt's version, written apparently about the middle of the present century—from a strictly New England point of view—of the exit of Peters from this mortal scene :

"With his face irradiated with the smile of heavenly assurance," says Peters' obstinate defender, "his spirit took its flight; and, as we trust, to become the subject of a *Commonwealth* liable to no change from human frailties, but ever dispensing its blissful benefits to the myriads within its jurisdiction."

This recalls a little anecdote recorded by Hume, in which the word we have italicised was introduced by a staunch Republican of 1641, *et seq.*, into the Lord's Prayer, to the exclusion of the word "kingdom." Mr. Felt's account, however, is, perhaps, taken from a partisan diurnal. If the living author of " The Great Civil War" does not moderate his views by the time he gets to the Restoration, it is possible he may, like Mr. Felt, treat Hugh Peters' end as heroic. We, with anti-Cromwellian prejudices, cannot go into ecstasies about regicides.

However sincere they may have been, we think the murderers of Charles I. were anything but heroes; and maintain that, upon the whole, never were criminals more leniently dealt with. The Jacobites at a later period were, with very much less criminality, far more severely treated. We do not refer to the barbarous penalties then in vogue for the punishment of high treason, but with regard to the numbers put to death. The Hanoverian vengeance, or shall we say Whig (?) was brutal. The Stuart King's last word* was a legacy of mercy. The living Hanoverian Sovereign does not come out of his triumph so well.

The large remnant of pugnacious Saints left alive in 1660-1 were, some of them, notwithstanding the compliments of Clarendon to the

* " Remember !"

disbanded army, extremely dangerous, and frequently tried to disturb order. Sir Walter Scott, in " Peveril of the Peak," seized and illustrated an incident. With regard to a later period, was there not something mysterious in the Great Fire of 1666? We all know that that disaster was subsequently set down falsely to the credit of the Catholics; and here the poet's lines may be remembered:

> Where London's column, pointing to the skies,
> Like a tall bully rears its head and *lies*.

But is it quite impossible that some violent veteran supporters of "the Good Old Cause" might have had something to do with it? The Great Fire, it may be remarked, broke out very nearly on the anniversary of St. Cromwell's Day—namely on September 2nd—and from the Diary of Pepys alone we seem to have evidence of some mysterious plot being suspected which could not be unravelled. Veteran Roundheads, seeing the relaxed state of manners which followed, and was indeed the result of their pretended saintly but really tyrannical reign, may have had bitter thoughts, and may (or probably did) cherish a revengeful spirit. A veteran fanatic who had seen men burnt to death in St. Peter's Church, Drogheda — for instance—would probably not regret to see "Paul's" in flames.*

In the year 1648 Oliver himself—enraged with the rampant reactionary spirit of the metropolis, which about the months of March, April, and May, 1648, was "all for the King," to the cry of "Down with the Parliament and Army!"—Cromwell, we say, was accused of formulating an incendiary threat.

"*What if it were for the glory of God,*" he is reported to have said, referring to London, "*if this city were burnt?*"†

A Royalist broadside chronicles this saying, and retorts with verses headed: "*Troy novant must not be burnt!*"

At present researches are made chiefly to discover the latent merits of the authors of the Great Rebellion and the supporters of the Commonwealth. A time might, of course, come, as we have already suggested, when *audi alteram partem* shall be the word. In that case the present idea might find an illustrator.

* In the month of April preceding the fire, some criminals, who do not appear to have been Catholics, confessed that there was a design to burn London.

† A threat to fire the city on Oliver's part is also mentioned in Walker's "History of Independency."

CHAPTER XXIV.

"In Memoriam."

The head of Hugh Peters was set up over the Surrey end of London Bridge, looking towards Kent and Surrey. That of his chief patron, Cromwell, as every one knows, was set up on Westminster Hall. It was, after many years, blown down in a storm, and being picked up by a soldier, eventually found its way into somebody's house in Kent. But the identity we know is disputed — there are, not other "Richards in the field," but other Oliver's heads, and some simple-minded showman, it is said, at one time exhibited a small skull which he asserted was that of Cromwell "when he was young."

Peters' wife seems to have remained insane and supported by charity. Appeals were made in her behalf to New England. Mr. J. B. Felt names a possible descendant of Peters' daughter having been heard of at Deptford—the "widow Barker."

One result of this little work may be, perhaps, further genealogical researches concerning pious Peters' posterity.

Peters' latest piece of writing, "A Father's Dying Legacy," is in one respect a parody upon the broadside containing the last words of the Royal Martyr to the poor young Princess Elizabeth (who died of grief at dreary Carisbrook Castle ; and to whom, in memory of her sad fate, our own Queen erected a monument in the church at Newport). King Charles advised his child to study Hooker. Peters also recommended his daughter to study "Hooker."

But the King's Hooker was the author of the "Ecclesiastical Polity," whose Fifth Book in defence of the Anglican Liturgy was the Charter and Palladium of the Anglican army of martyrs. The "Hooker" of Peters was the obscure Calvinistic pastor of New England.

Sir Thomas More jested upon the scaffold ; why not Hugh Peters in Newgate? Hugh Peters was always jesting ; sometimes, as in preaching against his Sovereign, his wit took a blasphemous turn. Possibly his levity, even with regard to the most serious matters, was irrepressible. The former "jester (or fool) of

Shakespeare's Company of Players" could not, perhaps, get out of the old groove.

A book was published which pretends to contain a number of his "original" jokes.

One to this effect:

"Beware, young men, of the three W's—Wine, Women, and Tobacco! Now tobacco, you will say, does not begin with a W. But what is tobacco but a weed?"

(Some may be surprised to learn that this synonym is so venerable.)

Another: "England will never prosper till one hundred and fifty are taken away."

The explanation is: " LLL, Lords, Lawyers, and Levites."

(Did Peters, at "the Globe," or "Blackfriars," or wherever his theatrical ministrations were, make a similar joke about "Love's Labours Lost"? Did he, or some other jester, call that play one hundred and fifty? And does not something of the spirit of the jest survive in "Kinahan's LL. Whisky"?

The sermons of Peters, which have been printed, are not funny—no doubt they were revised for "the press." One, in 1645, boasts of forty-two special providences since the year 1642.

They all are generally boastful of the visible favours of Heaven to "the Saints," and generally keep in view the necessity of increasing public plunder. Like other Puritanic discourses, they are divided into sections and subdivisions, first, to fifteenthly, etc.—all, as we said, more or less dull. But the actor would know when to introduce the amusing gag, which might scandalise were it seen in print. No doubt his grimaces were ludicrous. Perhaps he had been a diligent pupil of Thespis in early days.

But, indeed, exceptional humour, like poetic genius, is not made, but inborn. Pepys seems to admit having been amused by Peters. He speaks of a Scottish chaplain at Whitehall (after the Restoration), a Dr. Creeton, whose humour reminded him of Peters—"the most comical man that ever I heard; *just such a man as Hugh Peters.*" Dr. Creeton was, as Pepys reports, an unfriendly critic of Hugh Peters. "He ripped up Hugh Peters," says Pepys, "calling him the execrable Skellum,* his preaching stirring up the maids of the city to bring their bodkins and thimbles." But Marshal, Nye, Dell, Calamy, Burgess, and others were in the same category.

* "Skellum" is applied by Burns to Tam o'Shanter.

In the New England colony Peters must have had imitators. We have already mentioned that he has been boasted of by New Englanders as being "*the father of our commerce and the founder of our trade.*" It is not impossible, we think, that he may also have been the founder of American wit (!) His fun, we conceive, was, like all American fun, based upon exaggeration. He may have originated also the American business-like practice of contracting names. He, for instance, wrote Ipswich "Ips."

The nasal twang, which we sometimes hear in American talk, would be heard in his discourses, if not in his ordinary conversation. It was common to the Puritan party, and seems to have left an echo in East Anglia, the hotbed* of rebellious Puritanism. It was doubtless affected, though it had its uses. For in the pulpit or on the top of an inverted tub, the preacher who sang his discourse "through the nose." would be heard at a greater distance. Peters, as Cromwellian Primate, was head of the "Tryers," who decided whether candidates were up to the spiritual mark or not. One

* There was in East Anglia, as Mr. Kingston shows, a pretty considerable remnant of sturdy Royalists.

of his duties would be, according to Samuel Butler:

> To find in hue of beard and face
> The physiognomy of grace;
> And by the sound and twang of nose,
> If all be sound within disclose.

This is not the only mention by Butler's muse of a fashion thought to be becoming and pious (except by Royalists and Churchmen). "Sing it in the nose" is the preface to a burlesque rebel hymn. A Puritan *with a harp in his nose* is a phrase found in a Royalist pamphlet. Some roots of what we might call Yankee slang are seen in Peters' vocabulary. Sir John Birkenhead, editor of the first Tory newspaper, *Mercurius Aulicus*, 1642 *et seq.*, seems to think that Peters invented the very modern-sounding word "muchly," and another ugly slang phrase, Christ Jesus-ness (!)

It might be worth while for American literary inquirers to follow up the clue we have suggested.

It is strange that in the region where nasal song was loudest, viz., in New England, the purest English without any twang at all is now said to be spoken!

In concluding our remarks upon the sad

doings of one who is called by Mr. Gardiner "THE PRINCE OF ARMY CHAPLAINS," we shall mention a curious fact. We have suggested that the wit of Hugh Peters was based upon exaggeration. It is therefore not inappropriate to record that some of his sermons were printed and sold at the sign of the SPREAD EAGLE.*

* The Spread Eagle was also the family crest of John Milton. Had the great poet anything to do with patronising Peters' pious publications?

L'ENVOI.

WE now bid adieu to the wretched Hugh Peters, whose merits are enshrined in Mr. Gardiner's volumes and in the "National Biography." It is probable that what we have written may at present have no further result than to increase the sale of those works. Perhaps David Hume was correct in describing Hugh Peters as "mad." There was, however, method in his madness. Were not Cromwell, Ireton, and Harrison, and indeed the majority of the Puritan rebels also partly somewhat off their heads?* It used to be said that in North America the madhouses were chiefly tenanted by religious lunatics. The Puritan mother of the illustrious Bacon died religiously mad. The awful doctrines of the heartless Calvin are certainly calculated to upset the balance of the mind if fully accepted and much dwelt upon. Are we quite sure that they may not again,

* Scott, without saying as much, has shown that he thought so. Balfour of Burley and Cromwell had many ideas in common. Can anyone pronounce Balfour of Burley to be sane?

some day, as in the seventeenth century, take hold of masses of people, and revive the homicidal mania which Oliver Cromwell and his pugnacious Saints were not entirely free from, as well as the legend that they ought to *possess the earth?*

THE END.

APPENDIX A.

Letter of Thomas Peters, referred to at p. 36.

It is not worth while to quote it *in extenso*. It was written from Falmouth, June 26th, 1648. It mentions news which he must have got from the diurnals, viz., that King Charles "would wriggle out of the Castle," but, foreknown to Colonel Hammond, was taken "in the nick." Mentions Kentish rising, Colchester siege, and Pembroke (where his brother Hugh was with Cromwell). Hints the valuable prize Lord Capell will be — estate, twenty-four thousand pounds. Calls the Royalists "rogues," and the Scots "base all over," for invading England. The revolted fleet gone to Holland. "The chief commander is but a 'Botson's' mate" (alluding to Lendall). Concludes: "I send you two stones of lead thought to have silver in them. . . . The Lord Jesus advance this day of small things among you, and pray for your really affected *(sic)* friend, THO. PETERS."

APPENDIX B.

Hugh Peters.

From Gardiner's "Hist. Gt. Civil War."

Extracts from Mr. Gardiner's footnotes appear at the end of this quotation.

A man after Cromwell's own heart was Hugh Peters, the chaplain to the train—that is to say, to the regiments in charge of the baggage waggons and the artillery. Hugh Peters, who was born at Fowey, in Cornwall, 1598, was descended from a family which had emigrated from the Netherlands in consequence of religious persecution. He entered Trinity College, Cambridge, in 1613, at the age of fifteen. About 1620 he visited London, and was convinced of sin by a sermon which he heard at St. Paul's. Retiring to Essex, he fell under the influence of Thomas Hooker, and it was there that he married a widow, whose daughter by her first husband was afterwards the wife of the younger Winthrop. Upon his return to London he entered the ministry, and was licensed to preach by Bishop Montaigue. He became a lecturer at St. Sepulchre's, where, according to his own account, he preached to an overflowing congregation, and where "above a hundred every week were persuaded from sin to Christ." The days of Laud's influence were approaching, and shortly after Laud's translation to the See of London Peters found it expedient to remove to Rotterdam, where he became the minister of a Separatist congregation, and was not long in showing how little bigotry was in him. Both Ames, the English Separatist, and John Forbes, the Scottish Presbyterian, found in him a friend with whom they could converse on things which stand above the divisions of the Churches. Laud's arm, however, was long enough to reach Peters even in Rotterdam, and in 1635 the same ship which bore the younger Vane carried Peters to New England.

With Peters, who was soon engaged as a preacher at Salem, there was no impassable gulf between Divine things and the ordinary ways of human life. Never had any minister less of the professional clergyman than Peters. His letters show him as he really was—fond of a jest, much concernèd in the price of corn and butter, and taking the opportunity of a sermon to recommend the settlers to raise a stock for fishing, but anxious withal for the righteousness as well as for the material prosperity of the Colony. This idea of righteousness was not altogether in advance of his age. There had been a war with the Pequot Indians, and Peters had learned that captives had been taken. "We have heard," he wrote to Winthrop, "of a dividence of women and children in the Bay, and would be glad of a share, viz., a young woman or girl and a boy, if you think good."

Probably the children, if, as was very likely the case, their parents had been slain, would be better off in Peters' family than if they had been left to the chances of the woods. On another point, at least, he was altogether for self-sacrifice. "We are bold," he continued, "to impart our thoughts about the corn at Pequoit, which we wish were all cut down or left for the Naragansicks, rather than for us to take it; for we fear it will prove a snare thus to hunt after their goods whilst we come forth pretending only the doing of justice, and we believe it would strike more terror into the Indians so to do. It will never quit cost for us to keep it."

It is characteristic of the man that, although he was at one with Vane on the great question of religious liberty, he was shocked by the intolerant spirit of the party of toleration to which the young Governor had attached himself. He told Vane plainly that before he came the churches were at peace. Peters' love of liberty was not a high intellectual persuasion, like that of Vane or Milton, nor did it arise, like that of Roger Williams, from Biblical study, undertaken under the stress of persecution. It sprang from the kindliness of a man of genial temper, to whom minute theological study was repulsive, and who, without disguising his own opinions, preferred goodness of heart to rigidity of doctrine. Peters could not handle a religious subject without attempting to apply it in some way to the benefit of men of the world. These things he declared in his last apology for his life he had ever sought after: "First, that goodness, which is really so, and such religion might be highly advanced; secondly, that good learning might have all countenance;

thirdly, that there may not be a beggar in Israel—in England." With Peters, the difficulty was not to avoid quarrels, but to understand why men should quarrel. "Truly, it wounds my soul," he wrote at a time when, though the Civil War was at an end, ecclesiastical bitterness was at its height, "when I think Ireland would perish, and England continue her misery through the disagreement of ten or twenty learned men. . . . Could we but conquer each other's spirits, we should soon befool the devil and his instruments, to which end I could wish we that are ministers might pray together, eat and drink together ; because, if I mistake not, estrangement hath boiled us up to jealousy and hatred " (" Mr. Peters' Last Report ").

There must have been an absolute hostility to cant in a Puritan divine of the seventeenth century who could recommend dining* together as a remedy for the disputatiousness of the clergy. His own evident enjoyment of a good dinner, when it came in his way, led in the natural course of things to the charges which were brought against him by his enemies of being a glutton, if not something worse (see a satire entitled " Hosanna ").

Such was the man who, at the opening of the civil troubles, returned to England, and ultimately drifted into the position of an army chaplain in the New Model. It was a post for which he was emi-

---

* Lord Capell (the martyr) made some scathing remarks upon thanksgiving feasts (and " Roundhead banqueting " generally amongst the rebels). Did Peters, while enjoying "a good dinner," ever think of the thousands of starving, pious Anglican clergymen, who refused to break their oaths of allegiance and conformity, etc.?

nently fitted. It is easy to imagine how he could chat and jest with the soldiers, and yet could seize an opportunity to slip in a word on higher matters. His influence must have been such as Cromwell loved—an influence which in every word and every action made for concord. The wildest vagaries, the most rigid orthodoxy were equally secure of a mild and tolerant judgment from Peters. On the other hand, Peters was not the man to slacken the arms of the soldiers. For Royalism and the religion of Royalism he had a hearty detestation; and whenever there was a battle to be fought or a fortress to be stormed, he was always ready with a rousing appeal to the warriors of God's *(sic)* army (!) to quit themselves like men in the struggle against wickedness in high places. It was one of the saddest results of Laud's despotism that it had taught one who seemed born for the widest practical sympathy to regard the piety of the Church of England as absolutely outside the bounds of charity. Whatever judgment may be passed upon Peters, there can be no doubt that he was in high favour with Fairfax and Cromwell. It was Peters who had been selected to unfold at Westminster the tale of the surrender of Bridgewater; and he was now again employed to explain to Parliament, as an eye-witness only could explain, the full details of the surrender of Bristol.

Mr. Gardiner's Footnotes to the above.

1. The reputation of Hugh Peters has perhaps suffered more than that of any other man from the neglect of Mr. Spedding's dictum that if you wish to know whether a statement is true, you should ask

APPENDIX B.

who said it first, and what opportunity the sayer had of knowing the truth. The personal charges brought against him accused him of being a mountebank * and a loose liver. With respect to the former charge, there can be no doubt that he was fond of jesting, though it may be seen, by the MS. notes of his tales and jests in the B.M. (12,316 p. 5), that many of those ascribed to him were certainly, and many more probably in circulation before he was born. The other charge is more serious. Against the tales told after the Restoration, we have to set his own statement made to his daughter just before his death. "By my zeal, it seems, I have exposed myself to all manner of reproach; but I wish you to know that, beside your mother I have had no fellowship that way, with any woman since first I knew her, having a godly wife before also, I bless God" ("A Dying Father's Last Legacy"). The denial is not explicit concerning the writer's earlier years; but, on the other hand, it may be merely awkwardly expressed, Peters intending to refer to his first marriage, or it may be held to imply the acknowledgment of sins of his youth committed before conversion. Even if we take them in their best sense, there still remains the question whether Peters was speaking the truth. It is certain that the scribblers of the Restoration had no means of knowing whether Peters was guilty of committing adultery about thirty or forty years before they wrote, unless, indeed, it had become matter of public fame. Dr. Yonge only insinuates instead

* Mr. Gardiner chooses to ignore Dugdale, amongst others, who calls Peters "a pulpit buffoon." It is presumed that Burnet's complete condemnation of this Cromwellian "divine" is set down by Mr. Gardiner as slander.

of directly stating this ("England's Shame," 19); but he puts himself out of court by the assertion that Peters continued a lecturer at St. Sepulchre's for near twenty years, *i.e.*, from some date not much later than 1620 to nearly 1640—a statement notoriously untrue.* On the other hand, it may safely be said that a man who was treated as a friend by Thomas Hooker, Ames, Winthrop, and Cromwell cannot have been known as an evil liver. Even those who believed Cromwell to have been a hypocrite have never suggested that he was a fool; and what could be more foolish than for him to risk his reputation by giving his confidence to Peters, if his character had been no better than Royalist pamphleteers afterwards represented it?

If the evidence of *noscitur a sociis* is favourable to Peters, another line of evidence is also in his favour. A man may give a false account of his own life; but he cannot lie in those unconscious revelations of himself which spring to the surface when he is neither writing nor talking of himself. For this indirect knowledge of Peters' character there are three sources: (1) a series of letters written in America, and published in the collection of the "Massachusetts Historical Society," Series IV., Vol. VI., p. 91; (2) a sermon entitled "God's Doings and Man's Duty," preached on April 2nd, 1646 (E. 330, 11); and (3) "Mr. Peters' Last Report of the English Wars" (E. 351, 12). Unless I am mistaken, any candid reader of these will find that there is little difficulty in understanding

* Yet perhaps Peters was, during his long absence in Holland and America, *nominally* retained as "Lecturer" at St. Sepulchre's. After his return he seems to have frequently preached there.

the character of the writer, especially as the character here unconsciously drawn is just the one to give rise to the libellous attacks which have been made upon it. It is on these self-revelations that I have based my account of the man. In spelling the name I have adhered to the form Peters, which was usually adopted at the time, though in his own signature his name appears as Peter. The omission of the final "s" seems to have been a mere matter of habit, as in the cases of Bate for Bates, and Dyoe for Dyoes. I may add that Peters' last production, "A Dying Father's Last Legacy," appears to me a pious, sensible, and veracious work.

2. He was baptised June 11th, 1598. His father's name was Thomas Dyckwood, *alias* Peters ("Parochial Hist. Cornwall," II., 31).

3. He took his degree of B.A. from Trinity in 1617-18, and his M.A. in 1622 ("Felt's Memoir," and information supplied by Professor Mayer). The date of his birth contradicts the assertion of the Royalist pamphleteers, that he was a Fool in Shakespeare's Company.[*] His entry at Trinity is not given in the College registers, which do not notice the entry of pensioners so early; but his graduation at that College may be set against the statement of Dr. Yongè, in "England's Shame," that he was sent from school to the University of Cambridge, and there was admitted into Jesus College, and that being "obdurate and irrefragable to the civil government of that Collegiate Society," he was

[*] After Shakespeare's death the company might still have been called "Shakespeare's."

"expulsed the University." If writers blunder about matters concerning which the truth was ascertainable without difficulty, no credit is due to them when they tell us what passed in the bedroom of the first Mrs. Peters before her marriage.

Mr. Gardiner's tenderness for this pious Puritan "divine," the "man after Cromwell's own heart," may be instanced in two passages more. We might well quote the whole description of the sack of Basing House,* wherein Peters' patron, Cromwell, figures as "God's champion," having spent a great part of the night in meditation and prayer. (Here, as elsewhere, Mr. Gardiner faithfully follows the revered Carlyle.) Peters' "controversy with the Marquis of Winchester" is indexed, and found in Vol. II., p. 347. "The old man," writes Mr. Gardiner, had been stripped "of his costly attire," having had his life saved by Colonel Hammond.

Mr. Gardiner thus attempts to make some excuse for the brutal, un-Christian conduct of his "Prince of Army Chaplains."

"Consideration for fallen greatness never entered into the thoughts of a Puritan controversialist, even when that controversialist was of as kindly a dis-

* If the historian possesses a sense of humour he has not exhibited it in half excusing the murder of a girl by a soldier in these terms:—"One, a maiden of no ordinary beauty, a daughter of Dr. Griffith, an expelled City clergyman, hearing her father abused and maltreated, gave back angry words to his reviler. The incensed soldier, maddened with the excitement of the hour, struck her on the head, and laid her dead at her father's feet." But Peters thought this murder a moderate piece of slaughter: "*only one* woman," he mentions, was slain by the soldiers. Dr.(Matthew) Griffith had been favoured by the King, but had been deprived of his livings by the Parliament.

position as was Hugh Peters.* A Catholic, too, was beyond all bounds of religious courtesy; and Peters thought it well, as Cheynell had thought it well in the presence of the dying Chillingworth, to enter into argument with the fallen Marquis. "Did he not now see," he asked him, "the hopelessness of the cause he had maintained?" In such attempts at whitewashing, the ugliness of the idol becomes more distinctly visible.

The second passage from Mr. Gardiner's history which we must note places Peters in a still worse light. We italicise the historian's words (Mr. Gardiner's "History of the Great Civil War," Vol. III., p. 388).

"On Sunday, the 28th of January (1648 o.s.), he (King Charles) listened with a reverent devotion to the prayers of the Church read to him by Bishop Juxon, who had been allowed to visit him now that he was lying under sentence of death. . . . Words very different from those consolations . . . resounded on that Sunday morning in the chapel of Whitehall, where Hugh Peters preached before the High Court of Justice in justification of those who were seeking the King's death. *There was need of all his rude eloquence if those Judges, who had not yet given their signa-*

---

* We have shown how this "kindly disposition" did not prevent most un-Christian conduct towards the doomed Archbishop, whom Peters eventually replaced. As for Cheynell, we have already called him "detestable." The complete want of charity for men morally better than themselves, viz., for Episcopalians and Catholics who were on the King's side, makes the case of these violent Independents indefensible. The reign of "the Saints," as Sir Henry Maine observed, "*was never for one moment popular.*"

tures to the death-warrant, were to be steeled to the work before them" (!)*

---

* But, perhaps the historian, in this and similar passages, is only copying the supposed solemn, eccentric jocularity of Carlyle (see note at the end of chap. xx. of this book), however serious his words may appear.

www.ingramcontent.com/pod-product-compliance
Lightning Source LLC
Chambersburg PA
CBHW020830230426
43666CB00007B/1172